From Persia to America

The Life and Work of Emma Ordjanian Melikian

Stephen K. Batalden

The cover photo is of Emma Melikian at the Scottsdale, AZ office of her Thank You America Foundation, Mona Reeder, photographer, *Arizona Republic*—USA Today Network, 23 August 1998.

www.kendallhunt.com
Send all inquiries to:
4050 Westmark Drive
Dubuque, IA 52004-1840

Contents

Introduction

Embarking on a biography of Emma Ordjanian Melikian in late 2022, I was not unmindful of the complex worlds that Emma has bridged in her 90+ years, but I was unprepared for the level of complexity I would confront. Born in Tehran in the Imperial State of Iran during the worldwide Great Depression of the 1930s, Emma was the youngest child of a Russian-speaking Persian-Armenian family living in a predominantly Muslim country. Her formal schooling began in a classroom where Farsi was the language of instruction—Emma's second language alongside her third, Armenian. With a permit from Reza Shah, the first ruler of the Pahlavi dynasty, Emma's father built a thriving business in the production and distribution of vodka, zubrovka, and fine wines in a culture where consumption of alcoholic beverages was considered contrary to the teachings of the Quran. After emigrating to the United States, Emma ultimately became a champion of immigrants in a state (Arizona) where anti-immigrant rhetoric was invariably used for political advancement and anti-immigrant legislation was often the norm. The challenge of this biography has been to bring understanding to these and other seeming incongruities in the remarkable life and work of Emma Ordjanian Melikian.

"Life and work" in the subtitle borrows a phrase from the Russian, *"жизнь и творчество"* (zhizn' i tvorchestvo/life and work), used in biographical accounts where tvorchestvo, or work, carries the broader meaning of one's creative work or lifetime contribution. To place her far-ranging contributions in context, I have found it helpful to see Emma's work in the context of two significant interpretive issues of the twentieth and twenty-first centuries. The first of these is obviously that of modern American immigration history. Emma was an immigrant to America, arriving in 1948 from Iran. She was naturalized in 1954, the year of her wedding to Gregory Melikian. She often reflects on her own immigrant roots. While maintaining an appreciation for her Persian-Armenian heritage, she at the same time has sought patriotically to give back to her adopted American homeland. This immigrant experience places her squarely in the middle of a longstanding interpretive dispute over the nature of the immigrant experience in America.

On the one hand, post-World War II immigrant history was, for a generation and more, viewed through the prism of Oscar Handlin's seminal Pulitzer Prize-winning work, *The Uprooted.*[1] Who can forget Handlin's opening sentences:

> Once I thought to write a history of the immigrants in America.
> Then I discovered that the immigrants *were* American history.[2]

Setting aside the obvious slight to indigenous Native Americans who are also a part of American history, Handlin's magisterial work depicted the immigrant experience as one of alienation and dislocation. Immigrants had been uprooted from their European homeland and had to struggle to respond to the forces of secularization and modernization in urban America. Those forces would ultimately refashion immigrants into Americans, a process that some followers of Handlin framed as the "melting pot" of American society.

Critics of Handlin, however, argued that immigrants were not simply passive respondents to impersonal social forces in America, but were rather active in shaping their new society.[3] Newly arriving transplants, argued John Bodnar, were making real choices among options, drawing heavily upon the traditions of the homeland from which they had come, building communities that drew together like-minded citizens often from the same country of origin.

In this longstanding debate over the immigrant experience, the life of Emma Ordjanian Melikian provides a powerful testimonial on behalf of a

---

1. Oscar Handlin. *The Uprooted: The Epic Story of the Great Migrations That Made the American People* (Boston: Little, Brown & Co., 1951).
2. Ibid., p. 3.
3. See, for example, the work of John Bodnar, *The Transplanted: A History of Immigrants in Urban America* (Bloomington, IN: Indiana University Press, 1985).

post-melting pot perspective on the immigrant experience in post-World War II America. Emma and her extended family, including notably her brother Nikit, were empowered by their own Persian-Armenian roots. They built networks of support within their extended family and within the Armenian-American immigrant communities where they lived and worked. Those roots and those networks helped them refashion creative lives in America, even as they were guided by their own traditions in giving back to their respective communities. When Emma supported the building of two Armenian churches in America—one on Long Island and, later, one in Scottsdale, Arizona—she was honoring the community that had empowered her. Similarly, when she launched her non-profit organization in Phoenix, "Thank You America," it was to mobilize the diversity and strength of immigrant communities in Arizona. That she did this in the American southwest, the most heterogeneous region of the United States known for the demographic strength of its Native American and Hispanic populations—also the epicenter of reactionary anti-immigrant posturing—was even more noteworthy.

Study of the American immigrant experience has now also benefited from decades of work undertaken by social scientists who have been able to track more carefully the legal framework, statistics, and politics bearing on American immigration.[4] In the case of the Ordjanian family, their ability to emigrate from Persia to America was conditioned both by the changing legal environment and by a quota system arising out of that legal framework.

Attempting to limit immigration into the United States, the U.S. Congress in 1924 enacted the Johnson-Reed Act, known as the "Immigration Act of 1924." The terms of that act were very clear and racist. The law banned immigration from Asia and limited by quota the number of immigrants to be admitted annually to 165,000—a figure that was 80 percent less than the immigration quota operating prior to World War I. That figure was lowered to 150,000 in the 1927 revision of the 1924 act. The terms of the revised 1927 enactment also included a new quota system for each European country. The quota system was based on a calculation of the relative percentage of foreign-born U.S. citizens coming from each European country as documented in the 1920 census. That percentage was then used

---

4. The discussion of immigration legislation reflects the work of two scholars of U.S. immigration policy—Daniel J. Tichenor, *Dividing Lines: The Politics of Immigration Control in America* (Princeton, NJ: Princeton University Press, 2002), and Aristide R. Zolberg, *A Nation by Design: Immigration Policy in the Fashioning of America* (Cambridge: Harvard University Press, 2008).

to determine how many of the annual 150,0000 would be allocated to each European country. This quota system remained in place until the "Immigration and Nationality Act of 1965."

What these terms meant in practice can be seen in the case of immigrants from the United Kingdom. In the 1920 census, there were 89.5 million foreign-born U.S. citizens who had arrived in the United States from European countries. For the United Kingdom, roughly 44 percent of that number, or approximately 39 million U.S. citizens, claimed the UK as their country of origin. So, would-be immigrants from the United Kingdom could command up to about 44 percent of the 150,000 slots available annually for immigration into the United States. Such a system obviously favored preexisting patterns of U.S. immigration primarily from northern and western Europe. For East European nationalities with comparatively little representation among U.S foreign-born citizens, there was a minimal number allocated of 100 slots per country. Thus, Armenia was accorded 100 slots each year under the provisions of the 1924 Act as revised in 1927.

The problem for the Ordjanian family was not just that the number of Armenian slots was extremely low—one-hundred annually—but also that the Imperial State of Iran was counted among Asian countries from which immigration was banned. Fortunately for Emma's brother Nikit, who preceded the rest of the family to the United States in 1946, and then for the remainder of the family in 1948, Emma's father Samson could argue successfully before U.S. consular representatives in Tehran that the family had come from Russia, which was included within the quota system as a European state. Samson also needed to demonstrate that he had sufficient capital ($10,000 per family member) to assure that the family would not become a welfare burden, and another Persian-Armenian family, the Avakians, also had to provide assurances that the Ordjanians would be financially independent.

Owing to the considerable earlier immigration from Russia, including Jews from the Pale of Settlement and additional Russian immigrants arriving after the 1917 Revolution, the annual immigration quota for Russia, based on its percentage of foreign-born U.S. citizens in the 1920 census was 1.856 percent of the total. Out of the 150,000 allowable immigrants admitted annually, those coming from Russia could therefore command up to 2,784 slots (1.856% x 150K). Yet, owing to the virtual impossibility of out-migration from Stalin's Soviet Union, the 2,784 slots were under relatively less demand. Thus, one of the ironies of the cockamamie U.S. immigration quota system from the 1920s is that it facilitated Ordjanian emigration from Iran thanks to the quota for Russia, even though the family had earlier fled Russia following the release of Samson from imprisonment at the hands of Soviet authorities. The life and work of Emma Ordjanian Melikian needs to be understood in this context of the nuances of the immigrant experience and the history of American immigration policy.

The second major interpretive issue that is illumined in the life and work of Emma Ordjanian Melikian is that of the changing role of women in philanthropy. Throughout much of the nineteenth and twentieth centuries, in a world otherwise largely defined by gender inequality, women were empowered by their leadership in charitable social service agencies and by their activity in religiously-grounded orders and organizations serving those less fortunate—the poor, sick, hungry, and destitute.[5] While women's leadership in charitable organizations may at times have been seen as "auxiliary," lacking independent authority, the reality was that these charitable organizations became seedbeds for nascent feminism, leading to women's leadership in social action networks, not least of all the suffragist movement. Today, the place of women in philanthropy has exploded in importance, symbolized no doubt by the powerful role models of billionaire philanthropists Melinda French Gates and MacKenzie Scott. In the case of Melinda Gates, for example, her organization, Pivotal Ventures, founded in 2015, is seeking "to advance social progress in the United States by removing barriers that hold people back."[6] Among the projects launched by Pivotal Ventures is the $1 billion commitment to expand women's power and influence in the United States.

One of the challenges in writing about Emma Ordjanian Melikian is to identify where on the continuum of women and philanthropy she should be placed. Daughter of a generous entrepreneur-philanthropist who, among other contributions, helped establish the Armenian school in Sari, capital of the Mazandaran Province of Iran, Emma has never been hesitant to function be-

---

5. On earlier nineteenth-century women's charitable activity, see the standard accounts of F. K. Prochaska, *Women and Philanthropy in Nineteenth-Century England* (Oxford: Oxford University Press, 1980), and, for Russia, Adele Lindenmeyr, *Poverty Is Not a Vice: Charity, Society, and the State in Imperial Russia* (Princeton: Princeton University Press, 1996).

6. See the Pivotal Ventures website, https://www.pivotalventures.org/ (last accessed on 2/29/2024). See also Melinda Gates's own volume, *The Moment of Lift: How Empowering Women Changes the World* (Flatiron Books, 2019).

hind the scenes in the kind of charitable activity that requires rolling up one's sleeves and working in the trenches. She recalls the days she traveled around the Phoenix valley with Jerry Avakian seeking to gather enough funds from would-be donors to make the monthly mortgage payment for what became the St. Apkar Armenian Church and Cultural Center in Scottsdale. She was comfortable traveling to the CASS (Central Arizona Shelter Services) homeless shelter in downtown Phoenix to bring warm blankets. And she was enthralled by her meeting in Calcutta with Mother Theresa, one of the greatest examples of traditional religiously-grounded charitable activity.

But Emma Melikian has also been an independent entrepreneur-philanthropist in her own right. She kept her own bank accounts, and she was a full partner in the Melikian family real estate enterprise, maintaining her own real estate license and overseeing several remodeling projects for the business. Out of her own frugality, she managed to save funds she could donate directly to charitable institutions. At one point when her husband and partner Gregory thought it might be easier for all business accounts to function under his own signature alone, she quietly sought legal counsel, and was advised that she still had children to care for and that she ought to be careful about divesting herself of all signatory authority. Like her father and older brother before her, Emma has understood the importance of being able to exercise independence in matters of both business and philanthropy. While she has felt kinship with traditional women who brought leadership to charitable auxiliaries of old, she has been a strong woman who trusted her own independent judgment on matters of philanthropy. For the most part, Gregory has been willing to follow her lead.

This biography has benefited from more than six months of first-person interviews conducted weekly with Emma on Tuesday mornings. I also have had the opportunity to receive advice from Emma on much of the text. In that sense, this is, in part, an authorized biography. At the same time, both the interpretive issues outlined above and the choice of matters to include have been those of the author. As Emma's close friends and family know well, she is a woman whose generosity extends to all parts of her life, including her great love for family and friends. There are scores of such friends scattered throughout the U.S. and abroad, and Emma would of course want each of them to be included and praised in this recounting of her life and work. In the end, however, the inclusion or omission of people and events has been the burden of the author. Readers will find, for example, that there is greater detail surrounding the establishment of the Melikian Center than, for example, the work of Emma's non-profit foundation, "Thank You America." Those decisions over content invariably reflect the knowledge, as well as the limitations, of the author, who accepts full responsibility for the content. This is, in that sense, a biography, not an autobiography.

For her expertise as editor, I am indebted to my life partner, Sandra Batalden. The book is affectionately dedicated to a remarkable Persian-Armenian immigrant woman, American patriot, and philanthropist, Emma Ordjanian Melikian, who in her tenth decade continues to share her love of life with all those around her.

Note on Transliteration of Names

Because the family names of Emma Ordjanian Melikian's forebears were invariably written first in Armenian or Cyrillic, the names have quite naturally been rendered in a variety of transliterated or Romanized equivalents. This note, while it does not pretend to establish a new standard, nevertheless offers an explanation for the transliteration system used in this volume. As a general rule, except in the case of living family members whose own spelling of their names is used, the standard used throughout is that of Library of Congress transliteration from Cyrillic into English. Thus, Armenian family names commonly ending either in "ian" or "yan," have been transliterated, use the Romanized equivalent of the Cyrillic letter "я" as "ia." The result is that most Armenian names in the volume will end in "ian," rather than "yan."

Emma's maiden family name of Ordjanian has a particularly complicated history. The family came from northwesternmost Iran, near the Ottoman and Russian borders, where its original spelling was probably Ojaghian, or Ojaqian, spellings drawn from the Armenian root word for a blacksmith's hearth (*ojaq*). But Emma's father departed for the Russian Empire as a young man to work for his uncle in the Volga River city of Tsaritsyn. There he seems to have acquired the Russianized family name of Odjagov, or Odjakov. When in 1932 the family fled the Soviet Union for the Imperial State of Iran, as it came to be called, the family name probably reverted to Ojagian or Odjaghian. But, when the family received their Iranian passports the name was transcribed by Iranian authorities as "Ordjanian." That family spelling has remained standard for all the heirs of Samson in the United States, including Emma's brother Nikit Ordjanian and, of course, Emma Ordjanian Melikian. For simplification, I use Ordjanian throughout this account, even for the period when Emma's father Samson was in Russia. I have also accepted the English rendering of the first names of Samson's brothers—thus, Michael, not Mikhail; Daniel, not Daniil; and Armenak.

The transliteration of Emma Ordjanian Melikian's mother's family name is equally complicated. The Rustamian family hailed originally from the same northwestern Salmas region of Persia as the Ojaghian or Ordjanian family. But Emma's mother Maria Rustamian was born in Rostov (Rostov-na-Donu) on the Don River in Russia's southern steppe frontier where her family had relocated decades earlier. In Rostov, the family appears to have been known by the Russianized surname Rustamov (*Рустамов*). The successful family liquor production and distribution company that Samson led throughout southern Russia after marrying Maria was known as the Rustamov Brothers company. In his family memoir cited in this volume, Emma's brother Nikit transliterates his mother's Armenian family name as "Roostamian," Romanizing the Cyrillic "y" as "oo," not "u." I have followed the "Rustamian" spelling.

For Persian-Armenian families that have migrated from the Ottoman-Persian borderlands to Russia, then to Iran, and ultimately to the United States, there are bound to be differences in spelling of surnames. As in the case of Ordjanian, I have tried to use the spelling currently in use by families in the United States, recognizing that there may be equally appropriate spellings employed elsewhere.

Finally, I have adopted the more common current English spelling of the capital of Iran, Tehran, rather than its alternative, Teheran.

1

Family Origins – Russia

Emma Ordjanian Melikian was born in Tehran in 1933 into a Persian-Armenian family with longstanding ties to Iran, the South Caucasus, and the European Steppe frontier. The maternal Rustamian side of the family—her mother Maro, or Maria, was a Rustamian—traces its roots to Haftvan, a small multi-ethnic town in the Salmas region of northwestern Iran, near the Turkish and Armenian borders. Located close to the frontiers of the former Ottoman and Persian empires, Haftvan often felt the crossfire of violent upheavals.[1] It was a multi-ethnic community, predominantly Armenian, but with significant Assyrian Christian, Muslim Kurdish, and Azeri minorities. The thirteenth-century St. George Armenian Apostolic Church of Haftvan, still active as late as 2020, rested at the heart of the community.

---

1. Haftvan, today a town of about 6,500 people in Salmas County of Iran's West Azerbaijan Province, was in the nineteenth century a mixed Christian and Muslim village, with the Christian population composed of both Assyrian and Armenian communities. Its border status left it vulnerable to rival imperial armies. The most tragic event in the history of Haftvan occurred during the initial stages of what became the genocide directed against Assyrian and Armenian population by Ottoman armies. In early 1915, under the guise of requiring the Assyrian and Armenian population to register for wartime food rations, the occupying Ottoman forces executed more than seven-hundred male heads of households gathered in the town center. By 1915, both the Rustamian and Ordjanian families had migrated to the Russian Empire, thereby escaping the slaughter. Though she never visited the town when she was a young girl living in Tehran, Emma notes that the Ordjanian side of her family left property in Haftvan only some of which was later disposed of when the family was in Tehran.

Haftvan, Iran[2]

**Thirteenth-century Armenian Church of
St. George in central Haftvan**[3]

---

2. Red dot denotes location of Haftvan. Google Maps (2024) Haftvan, Iran, 1":400mi. Available from https://www.google.com/maps/place/Haftvan,+West+Azerbaijan+Province ,+Iran/@34.8845396,42.6940088,5z/data=!4m6!3m5!1s0x4011b216a1a1009d:0x67ec405b-69440ba0!8m2!3d38.168187!4d44.7582683!16s%2Fm%2F0yp005g?entry=ttu, accessed 23 February 2024.

3. "St. George Church, Haftvan," *Wikipedia* (https://en.wikipedia.org/wiki/St._George_Church,_Haftvan, last accessed on 23 February 2024).

Emma's maternal grandfather, Hovhannes Rustamian (1841-1915), left Haftvan sometime in the latter half of the nineteenth century to pursue his fortune in the Russian Empire, traveling to the Steppe city of Rostov on the Don River (see map below). There he became a successful merchant, producer, and retailer of beer and fine wines, and the owner of Rostov's most popular delicatessen.[4] It was there that Emma's mother Maro, or Maria as she came to be called, was born in 1896.

Map of the southern Steppe with Rostov-on-Don immediately east of the Sea of Azov; Tsaritsyn/Volgograd on the lower Volga River that empties into the Caspian Sea, lower right.[5]

4. Rostov-on-Don, the capital of the Rostov oblast in the Southern Federal District of Russia on the lower Don River, is a predominantly Russian city located close to the border of the occupied Ukrainian Donbas, and perilously close to the scene of current Russian-Ukrainian fighting. Rostov was a logical destination for Armenians arriving from the south because of the large Armenian community that already populated the adjoining town of Nakhichevan, also on the Don. Nakhichevan was established in 1779 by Armenians who were evacuated from the Crimean peninsula at the urging of Russian Empress Catherine II. The Empress sought to weaken the Crimean Khan by granting land and tax incentives to evacuating Armenians prior to Russia's military annexation of the Crimea in 1783. Today, with a population of more than one million, the merged cities of Rostov-on-Don and Nakhichevan constitute the tenth largest city of the Russian Federation. The Rustamian delicatessen was located on the major Rostov boulevard, Pushkinskaia Ulitsa [Pushkin Street], in the center of the city. Situated on a northeast-to-southwest line, Pushkinskaia Ulitsa runs parallel to the Don River, which is one kilometer to the south. The street has to this day a fashionable midway dividing traffic flowing in either direction.
5. Google Maps [2024] Rostov-on-Don. 1":200 mi. Available from https://www.google. com/maps/place/Rostov-on-Don,+Rostov+Oblast,+Russia/@47.2610019,38.3095694,6z/ data=!4m6!3m5!1s0x40e3c777c3b4b6ef:0x8248b451e48b4d04!8m2!3d47.2357137! 4d39.701505!16zL20vMDF2MTVm?entry=ttu (accessed 23 February 2024).

The paternal side of Emma's family—the Ojaghian, Odjagov, or Ordjanian family[6]—also had its origins in the town of Haftvan. Emma's paternal grandparents, Mkrtich and Nubar, remained in Haftvan. But, their eldest son and the future father of Emma, Samson (1889-1955), was sent in 1901 at the age of twelve to work for an uncle in the distant Russian Volga River city of Tsaritsyn (see map above).[7]

Following the death of both his parents from tuberculosis in 1907, Samson was joined in Tsaritsyn by three younger brothers, Mikhail/Michael, Daniil/Daniel, and Armenak. According to the memoir issued by Emma's brother Nikit, the enterprising young Samson, while tending to the needs of his brothers, launched his own business when he was just twenty years old. Much of his business, as Emma recounts, entailed import/export trade for which he would travel widely. Emma notes hearing about her father's early travels when he would purchase furniture, textiles, and other household goods from as far away as Warsaw and Moscow. By the outbreak of World War I, Samson's business was thriving, leading to the purchase of his own home in Tsaritsyn in 1915 where he lived with his three brothers.

Sometime prior to 1916, Samson was introduced through a distant relative to a young pre-med student in Rostov-on-Don, Maria Rustamian, who was barely twenty years old at the time. Possibly fueled by peer influence—she socialized with a talented, multi-ethnic group of neighborhood Russian, Jewish, and Armenian female student friends—Maria wished to become a doctor, a goal that was attainable for women in Russia at the time. By 1914, Russian medical faculties were graduating more than one thousand women per year, many in Rostov.[8] In Rostov the Ministry of Education in 1916 had formally established a Medical Institute for Women, which was located close to Pushkinskaia Ulitsa and the Rustamian delicatessen. That Women's Institute was later merged with the Rostov State Medical University, one of today's leading medical training institutions in the Russian Federation.

---

6. See the introductory "Note on the Transliteration of Names" above.
7. This account of Samson and the Ordjanian family draws not just on the personal reminiscences of Emma Melikian, but also the unpublished family history written by Emma's brother, Nikit Ordjanian, "To Anahid and Armen with Love," New York, 1988/1989, 70pp.
8. Ruth Dudgeon, "The Forgotten Minority: Women Students in Imperial Russia, 1872-1917," *Russian History*, vol. 9, no. 1 (1982), p. 13.

The Rustamian family in Rostov-on-Don on the eve of World War I. Maria is standing third from the left. Her mother (Shohokat) and father (Hovhannes) are seated to the left of the table (photo, courtesy of the Ordjanian family, is from the private album of Armen Elliot, Emma Melikian's niece).

Whether from family considerations—Maria's father had died in 1915—or from romantic love, or both, Maria Rustamian married the enterprising Haftvan native, Samson Odjagov (Ordjanian), in a wartime wedding ceremony held in Moscow in May 1916 and presided over by Fr. Artem Simonian. Simonian was the same priest who, thirty-eight years later after having migrated to New York City, would marry Emma and Gregory Melikian.

After the marriage, Maria joined Samson in Tsaritsyn where, as her son Nikit would later put it, "the young housewife Maria presided over a household of four brothers and a couple of servants."[9] Emma relates that

Wedding photo [damaged] of Samson and Maria (Moscow, 1916), from the private album of Armen Elliot, courtesy of the Ordjanian family

9. Nikit Ordjanian, "To Anahid and Armen with Love," p. 5.

her father Samson had specifically indicated at the time of his engagement that he wanted his younger brothers to continue to live with the family in their transplanted Tsaritsyn home.

Maria (on the right) pictured here in Tsaritsyn with two of Samson's brothers, Daniil (left) and Armenak (right). Photo is from the album of Armen Elliot, courtesy of the Ordjanian family.

There followed in Tsaritsyn the birth in 1917 of a first son, Emma's brother Mkrtich (subsequently Russified as Nikita, or Nikit), and a daughter, Isabella, in 1918. These significant family events came at a time when the Russian Empire was undergoing a profound reorientation accompanying the initial February 1917 Revolution and the subsequent October 1917 Bolshevik Revolution. Nikit notes in his memoir that Maria, who "was more to the political left than most of her contemporaries," welcomed the February Revolution, the abdication of Nicholas II, and the end of tsarist autocracy.[10] But, the Bolshevik Revolution and the Russian Civil War that followed not only undermined the Odjagov enterprise in Tsaritsyn, but they also led to the imprisonment and a death sentence for the young family patriarch Samson, who was viewed as a propertied capitalist, something anathema to the new regime. The birth of Isabella in July 1918 came during the height of the violent Civil War between the Red and White armies in the city of Tsaritsyn. Maria successfully persuaded (or possibly bribed?) the Bolshevik authorities in Tsaritsyn to release her husband, aid-

---

10. Nikit Ordjanian, "To Anahid and Armen with Love," p. 7.

ed no doubt by the argument that he was, after all, a documented citizen of Persia, not Russia, and therefore could argue for international immunity. Despite Samson's release and freedom from incarceration, the family decided to abandon Tsaritsyn and flee for the remainder of the Civil War to the more remote mountainous location of Kislovodsk in the Stavropol region on the north Caucasus slopes.

In 1918, the city of Tsaritsyn, where the Ordjanians had resided, became one of the epicenters of the Russian Civil War. Tsaritsyn was early on taken over by the Bolsheviks for whom the industrialized city with its munitions factories and connecting railways was a critical hub providing goods to Moscow from Central Asia and the lower Volga. Under the military command of Bolshevik General Kliment Voroshilov, and aided by Joseph Stalin who arrived in the city in June 1918, Red Army forces held off three separate campaigns directed against the city by anti-Bolshevik White forces comprised of 40-50,000 Don Cossacks under the command of their Cossack Ataman Pëtr Krasnov. After cutting off adjoining rail lines, the Cossacks finally managed to seize Tsaritsyn in 1919, resisting the Red Army until the city fell to the Bolsheviks once again in 1920. The renaming of the city as Stalingrad in 1925 (it was again renamed Volgograd in 1961) reflected the role played by Stalin as one of the leaders in the Bolshevik defense of Tsaritsyn. Amidst this chaotic back and forth fighting, the Odjagov family managed a harrowing escape from Tsaritsyn and an equally harrowing transit to Kislovodsk.

Kislovodsk, a modestly-sized north Caucasus city known for its natural mineral springs and spas, was a regional vacationing center. Having been established as a municipality in 1903, its growing population of approximately 50,000 included a significant Armenian minority that included Samson's distant relatives from Haftvan, the Avakians. Samson and his brothers managed to do reasonably well in the new environment, even amidst the ongoing Civil War, establishing a soap manufacturing company adjacent to the spas. Kislovodsk was also the birthplace of Alexander Solzhenitsyn (1918), who spent his childhood there. Alexander Solzhenitsyn's mother, Taisiia Zakharovna, had studied in Moscow before marrying an Imperial Russian army officer and returning to her native surroundings of the north Caucasus. It is interesting to speculate whether the two young mothers, Maria Odjagova and Taisiia Solzhenitsyna, and their respective young charges of the same age ever encountered each other in the streets and nurseries of Kislovodsk.

By 1921, the Civil War had ended, and the Bolsheviks had secured power throughout the Caucasus Mountain region, as well as in Ukraine and along the European Steppe frontier. With renewed opportunity for entrepreneurial activity occasioned by Vladimir Lenin's New Economic Policy (NEP), Samson and Maria decided to return to the Steppe, though not to Stalingrad (Tsaritsyn/Volgograd) where Samson had been imprisoned, but rather to Rostov-on-Don, where the Rustamian delicatessen had managed to survive. The family settled in a six- room flat on Pushkinskaia Ulitsa in Rostov where they would spend the rest of the 1920s. A third child, Emma's brother Ashot, was born in 1922.

Emma's brothers and sister were all born in Russia. From left to right: Nikit (1917, Tsaritsyn), Isabella (1918, Tsaritsyn), and Ashot (1922, Rostov-on-Don). Photo is from the private album of Armen Elliot, courtesy of the Ordjanian family.

In Rostov-on-Don, Samson joined as a partner in—and later headed—a wine and liquor factory started by two of Maria's brothers, Zakhar and Aram Rustamian. As Nikit describes it, the firm, named the "Rustamov Brothers," was by 1925 "a well-known entity in the entire north Caucasian region—i.e., southern European Russia." He writes, "These were years when successful businessmen maintained dachas, horse-driven carriages, nannies and governesses for their children, and led lives not much different from the preWorld War I imperial times." The Rustamov Brothers firm was large enough to support workers from more than two hundred families.[11]

All that changed with the arrest of Samson in January 1930. Reflecting the wider post-NEP Stalinist crackdown on bourgeois merchants and kulaks, the charge against Samson was that he was "an enemy of the people,"

---

11. Nikit, "To Anahid and Armen with Love, p. 10

a private capitalist exploiting workers. He was incarcerated in the nearby city of Novocherkassk, and the family lost most of its possessions, no longer able to maintain domestic help, tutors, or music teachers. In retrospect, Emma likens the fate of her family to that described in Boris Pasternak's *Dr. Zhivago*—families dispossessed by Bolshevik state expropriation of private family holdings. To protect her family, which could be charged with guilt by association, Maria officially divorced her husband and took day labor as a seamstress. Behind the scenes, she bribed prison officials so that Samson not be sent to the Gulag. She also traveled multiple times to Moscow, seeking through intermediaries to present the justice of Samson's case to Communist Party officials—Samson was, after all, an honest businessman following legal Soviet policies under Lenin's NEP.

At one time, in 1930, it appeared as though Samson would be exiled with one hundred other political prisoners from Novocherkassk to Siberia, but Maria claims that one of the workers in the Rustamov Brothers brewery managed a timely intervention with the authorities to defend the integrity of Samson, such that Samson's name was placed in position no. 101 on a list of one hundred bound for exile to Siberia. He was saved from banishment to the Gulag. In the end, Maria's success in getting the Central Committee of the Communist Party to release Samson in late 1931 may well have been owing also to the intervention of her brother-in-law, Gurgen Apressov. Apressov, who was married to Maria's youngest sister Elizabet (Liza), had a brother who was a high-ranking Party leader in the region. That brother-in-law probably managed to intercede with the Communist Party Central Committee to secure Samson's release from the Novocherkassk prison in late 1931. As part of the terms of his release and exoneration, Samson was invited to take a position with a brandy company near Moscow. No doubt persuaded by Maria, Samson decided that it would be best to use his status as a Persian subject, and the exit opportunity his documents afforded, to reestablish his family in Iran.

In January 1932, Samson and Maria, along with their children Nikit, Isabella, and Ashot, departed the Soviet Union by ship on the Caspian Sea, arriving at the largest southern Caspian port city of Bandar-e-Anzali (renamed Bandar-e-Pahlavi during the rule of the Pahlavi dynasty) in Iran. The exodus of Samson and family to Persia was preceded by the departure for Tehran of Maria's mother, Shohokat, who had left Rostov-on-Don shortly before with one of Maria's brothers. Maria's father Hovhannes had earlier died in Rostov-on-Don in 1915.

What are we to make of this family into which Emma would soon be born? They had obviously experienced trauma and persecution. The trials of their life on the European Steppe involved not one but two incarcerations, family separations, the extremes of affluence and deprivation, and the violence of revolution and civil war. What stands out as remarkable about the family, and about Samson in particular, is the unprecedented mobility that marked their life. At the age of twelve Samson had traveled from Haftvan to Tsaritsyn where he developed his own import/export business that entailed yet further extensive travel throughout the Russian Empire, including but not limited to Warsaw and Moscow. When he then married a young woman from Rostov-on-Don, Maria Rustamian, the marriage took place not in Rostov-on-Don, but in Moscow. Once back in Tsaritsyn, he was forced to flee with his family to Kislovodsk during the harrowing years of the Civil War, but then returned to affluence in Rostov-on-Don, and joined the Rustamian brothers as head of their thriving brewery. At a time when ninety percent of the population lived and died without ever moving more than thirty kilometers from their place of birth, this was a remarkable, though not unique, phenomenon, aided as it was by new forms of transport, especially the railway and, in time, the automobile.

As Benedict Anderson noted long ago in his classic study of the origins of nationalism, these were not only highly mobile entrepreneurs—the spontaneous multipliers of production, and of productivity—they were the harbingers of "modernity."[12] Many of the old traditions remained, but it was into this distinctly modern, highly mobile Persian-Armenian family that Emma would be born in 1933.

Emma's father, Samson Odjagov/ Ojaghian/Ordjanian (1889-1955). The photo dates from his years in Persia following imprisonment in Novocherkassk and migration to Tehran in 1932. Photo is from the Melikian family archive.

12. Benedict Anderson, *Imagined Communities: Reflections on the Origin and Spread of Nationalism* (London: Verso, 1983).

2

Persia – Tehran and Mazandaran

The Imperial State of Persia to which the Odjagov/Ordjanian family migrated in 1932 was undergoing profound economic and political transformation. The 1917 Russian Revolution had unleashed a series of challenges to Qajar imperial rule in Persia. The revolutionary Bolshevik government initially occupied a portion of northwesternmost Persia, declaring the establishment of the Persian Socialist Soviet Republic (or Socialist Soviet Republic of Gilan). For its part, Britain, in defense of its Anglo-Persian Oil Company interests, sent its armed forces into Persia with an eye toward supporting White armies in the Russian civil war. Weakened by these competing international interventions and hamstrung by the lack of central authority, the last of the Qajar dynasts, Ahmad Shah, was deposed in a 1921 military coup led by an ambitious young colonel in the Iranian army, Reza Khan. With British backing, Reza Khan would ultimately consolidate power, assuming initially the position of war minister in the new government. A Russo-Persian Treaty of Friendship, signed in Moscow in 1921, managed also to secure, at least for a time, the withdrawal of the Soviet Union from occupied Persian territory.[1]

On 15 December 1925, the Grand Majlis, or consultative assembly of local representatives, formally designated Reza Khan as first *shah* of the House of Pahlavi (Reza Shah Pahlavi) in the new Imperial State of Iran. Although Reza Pahlavi (1878-1944) was an autocratic leader, his autocracy

---

1. On modern Iranian history up to 1979, see P. Avery, G. R. G. Hambly, & C. Melville, eds., *The Cambridge History of Iran*, vol. 7 (Cambridge: Cambridge University Press, 1991).

combined firm military rule with a program of state modernization that offered opportunities for enterprising non-Muslim populations, including the approximately 200,000 Persian Armenians who had settled in Persia in the early twentieth century.

For centuries there had been a substantial Armenian population in Persia, especially in the northwestern region of Salmas (in what was called the West Azerbaijan Province of Iran), as well as in the cities of Isfahan, Tabriz, and Tehran. But the rapid growth of the Armenian population in the interwar Imperial State of Persia, or Iran, was owing to a set of profoundly tragic events affecting the legacy of the Armenian people. As many as 50,000 future Persian Armenians were among those forced to flee genocide at the hands of the Ottoman government during World War I. Another 10,000 Armenians, largely the defeated Dashnaks (the Dashnaktsutyun, or Armenian Revolutionary Federation), fled the Soviet Union following the Red Army's victory over the fledgling Democratic Republic of Armenia (1918-1920). The nationalist Dashnaks would continue to play a prominent role in Persian Armenian politics throughout the interwar period. Finally, there were another 30,000 Armenians, including the Ordjanians, who fled the Soviet Union in the years prior to Soviet border closure in 1933. The result of these politically forced migrations was a virtual doubling of Persian Armenian population in Iran by the time the Ordjanians settled in Tehran in 1932.

The five Ordjanian family members who landed in the port city of Bandar Anzali (Pahlavi) in January 1932—Emma's parents Samson and Maria, and her three siblings (Nikit, Isabella, and Ashot)—were arriving in what was for the younger generation *terra incognito*. Her brother Nikit recalls the wonders of their arrival:

> Although father left Rostov practically broke, he still had a few gold coins somewhere hidden on him. He promptly exchanged them for Iranian currency and bought sweets, fruits, and other delicacies of which we could only dream during the previous year in Rostov. It was also the first time in our lives that we saw, outside of a circus, live caravans of camels, which at that time were the chief means of cargo transportation in Iran. In sharp contrast to the cold and snow-covered streets of Rostov in January, we enjoyed the sunny streets of Pahlavi with their colorful displays of all kinds of goods (all scarce commodities in the USSR) and

Persian rugs and carpets on sale. Also for the first time we realized that we were now part of a different culture when we heard the callings and prayers of mullahs from the minaret towers of numerous mesheds [holy shrines] in the city, and mingled in the streets with heavily veiled women in black chadors.[2]

This Google map of northern Iran includes the port city of Bandar Anzali, renamed Bandar Pahlavi after 1925, as well as the northwest region of Salmas near Lake Urmia, and the capital city of Tehran immediately south of the Caspian Sea. Just south of the Caspian Sea toward the far eastern section of the map is the Persian town of Sari, where Samson established his brewery. The red dot denotes the seaside town of Babolsar where the Ordjanians often spent summers by the sea.[3]

By cab the family traveled some days later to Tehran where they stayed briefly in a hotel before renting an apartment in the city. During that first year in Tehran the family was sustained not only by the gold that they had managed to conceal in their belongings during their travel to Iran, but by savings Samson had transmitted to the Avakian family in Tabriz—monies accumulated from his successful days with the "Rustamov Brothers" brewery in Rostov.[4] Those savings, combined with credit generously offered by friends who knew Samson's reputation from his days in Rostov-on-Don,

2. Nikit Ordjanian, "To Anahid and Armen with Love" (New York, 1988/89), p. 15
3. Google Maps [2024] Northern Iran. 1":100 mi. Available from https://www.google.com/maps/place/Iran/@37.1751478,49.2527908,7z/data=!4m6!3m5!1s0x3ef7ec2ec16b1d-f1:0x40b095d39e51face!8m2!3d32.427908!4d53.688046!16zL20vMDNzaHA?entry=ttu (accessed 3 March 2024).
4. Nikit Ordjanian, "To Anahid and Armen with Love" (New York, 1988/89), p. 15.

allowed Samson both to settle his family in Tehran and to start new enterprises, including a brewery and vodka distillery, as well as a small chocolate factory in the basement of their newly purchased home. Emma notes that in those first years in Tehran when the family was living in more modest circumstances her mother Maria added to the family income by selling some of her own artfully crafted handwork that she sewed in the evenings.

It was in that newly adopted Tehran setting that Maria, already 36-years of age, unexpectedly became pregnant with Emma. The other children—Nikit, Isabella, and Ashot—were already 16, 14, and 11, respectively, and Maria was apparently uneasy about the unplanned pregnancy. Because of Maria's age and the family's limited resources, there was apparently some consideration given to aborting the pregnancy—a common form of birth control that Maria had apparently used in the past. But Maria was already well along in the pregnancy and was advised by a family physician, Dr. Hamzedi, to carry the baby to term. Emma was born on 4 April 1933, less than fifteen months after the family's arrival in Tehran. The labor was particularly difficult, and Maria was fortunate to survive. According to Nikit, all three of Emma's siblings were initially unhappy about this addition to the family, probably worrying over their mother's health. But Samson from the very beginning greeted the birth with unbridled joy, saying, "God provided us with Emma, and God will provide for her."[5]

Emma's Early Years

Emma's memory of her early childhood is one of a loving household, whose residence was a center for happy extended family gatherings and rigorous tutorial training. As the youngest child separated from her siblings by more than ten years, Emma drew the loving attention of her older brothers, as well as her sister Bella, who occasionally seemed as much a second mother as a sister. The family doted on Nikit, whose German governess also served as a tutor in German. While attending the French Lyceum in Tehran (Lycée Franco-Persan), Nikit would also be tutored in Farsi. The family spoke Russian at home, and Emma's first language was Russian. For all the attention accorded her older brother, Emma noted that "Bella was the leader in our family." Isabella would not only assist her mother in caring for Emma, but she was a gifted seamstress in her own right who of-

---

5. Ibid., p. 17.

ten designed clothes for friends and family on the Singer sewing machine purchased for her. On top of that, Bella was an accomplished young pianist, whose musical talent would be featured in Sunday afternoon performances held at the Ordjanian family home in Tehran virtually every month.

Ordjanian Family in Teheran 1936. From left: Emma, Samson, Isabella, Ashot, Maria, and Nikit. Photo from Melikian Family Archive.

Emma's younger brother, Ashot, was the weaker, more sickly family member, whose health had been compromised at the early age of five (1927) in a case of scarlet fever that was "misdiagnosed and mistreated by local physicians in the resort city of Sochi on the Black Sea," leaving him with kidney problems that would take his life at the age of sixteen.[6] Emma was just five years old when Ashot died. What she recalls most vividly about Ashot was his love of opera. "Every day we would hear opera at our house," Emma recalls, "and I owe my love of opera to Ashot."

The Sunday musical events would be attended by the wider extended family, many of whom also regularly graced the Ordjanian table for dinner—a table set with fine china, one of the legacies of the years in Rostov-on-Don. From both the Rustamian and Ordjanian sides, many of the families closest to Maria and Samson had gravitated to Iran from the Soviet Union in the 1930s. On the Rustamian side, Maria's brother Zakhar and his family had fled in 1932, the same year as the Ordjanians. Zakhar oversaw a brewery in Tehran. Maria's brother Aram and family had also preceded

---

6. Ibid., p. 30.

the 1932 Ordjanian family arrival. Several other refugees followed later in the 1930s, including Maria's sister Susanna and Susanna's daughter Anahid (Ida). Susanna had been recently widowed, her husband having died in a Russian prison camp. The Rustamian family naturally gravitated to the Ordjanian home in Tehran because the matriarch of the family, Emma's maternal grandmother Shohokat, maintained her residence with the Ordjanian family until her death on the eve of World War II.

On the Ordjanian side, Samson's brother Mikhail (Misha) arrived with his wife Elizabet (Liza), and opened a delicatessen in Tehran. Another brother Armenak arrived with family, and stayed in Razvin where they opened their own winery. Samson's third brother, Daniil, had died in 1930. All these relatives and other more distant family and friends took their turns at the Ordjanian table in Tehran. To manage all these occasional visits, Emma's mother hired several assistants, including governesses for Nikit and Bella, and "four young Armenian girls from the Salmas region," as Emma describes them, who would assist with meal preparation and household chores.

Among those at the Ordjanian family table in Tehran were the members of the extended Ordjanian/Odjagov family in Teheran pictured here in 1940. Standing left to right: Rafik, Michael (Samson's brother), Nubar (Luba), Mark Davidian, Isabella (Emma's sister), Samson, Armenak (Samson's brother), and Alexander. Seated from left: Elizabet (Liza, wife of Michael), Maria (Emma's mother), & Ashkhen. On floor from the left: Emma and Evelyn. Not pictured is Nikit (Emma's older brother), who was pursuing advanced studies in Europe. Photo is from a private album of Armen Elliott, and is provided courtesy of the Ordjanian family.

The Sunday musical events were in some sense Maria's compensation for the Rustamian family's bitter loss of its former Steinway grand piano—one of only two in Rostov-on-Don—which was confiscated by Bolshevik authorities shortly after the Russian Revolution. Emma recalls hearing the account of property confiscation and other stories of the tribulations visited on the Rustamians at the hands of the Bolsheviks. Such stories must have been repeated often at the Ordjanian table in Tehran, filled as it was with Russian-Armenian emigres fleeing the Soviet Union.

Housing in Tehran

The earliest housing that Emma recalls is the two-story apartment occupied by the Ordjanians in a U-shaped building that it shared in central Tehran with the celebrated Persian-Armenian architect, Gabriel Guevrekian (1900-1970).[7] Guevrekian, one of the premier modernists in European architecture, had his residence on one of the floors not occupied by the Ordjanian family. Emma describes the home as having two curved staircases opening onto their second-floor balcony entry. The family dining table, set on the balcony between the two staircases, seated twenty-four people. She added, "I don't ever remember being at the long dining table without extended family; our table was always full." Later the family moved to a unit on Koutche Laleh #11 in central Tehran close to the American School. During World War II, the family moved a third time to their own detached house just around the corner from the Koutche Laleh residence.

From the architect Guevrekian the Ordjanians inherited their dog, "Shangul," a greyhound that was very much devoted to Emma's brother

---

7. Born in Istanbul, Guevrekian grew up in Tehran and then moved to Vienna to study architecture at the Kunstgewerbeschule. He later worked with Oskar Strand, Josef Hoffmann, Adolf Loos, Henri Sauvage, and Robert Mallet-Stevens. Among his most famous designs are the Cubist garden for Villa Noailles in France and two houses for the Vienna Werkbund exhibition. Not yet thirty, Guevrekian was recognized as one of the early protagonists of the European Avant-garde in Paris. During the 1930s, he was invited back to Iran where he served as chief architect for the city of Tehran, designing public buildings and several homes. After the Second World War, he took teaching posts in Europe and America, notably for the last twenty years at the University of Illinois where his personal papers are preserved in the University Library. See Hamed Khosravi, *The Elusive Modernist: Gabriel Guevrekian,* Berlin: Hatje Cantz, 2020. See also Mina Marefat, "Building to Power: Architecture of Tehran, 1921-1941," Ph.D. diss., Massachusetts Institute of Technology, Cambridge, 1988.

Ashot. Emma recalls how, at the time of Ashot's death in 1937, Shangul remained alongside the casket, and seemed to remember Ashot on visits to the grave where the dog would remain for lengthy periods without eating. Following the death of Ashot, Emma inherited Shangul, who often slept at night under her bed.

Tall for her age of five, Emma is pictured here with Shangul on one of the two matching staircases leading to the entry into her home in Tehran. Photo is from the Melikian Family Archive.

Early Education

Like her brothers and sister, Emma was tutored at home even before beginning her formal education. She started formal schooling in a private kindergarten, from which her sister Bella would "rescue" her every afternoon. Her tutor at home was a Russian teacher by the name of Gospodin Bulgakov (Mr. Bulgakov). Bulgakov effectively home-schooled Emma each afternoon, even coming after Emma began going to local schools. Bulgakov would provide math, science, and literature lessons, all in Russian. Emma was also tutored separately in Armenian and French. For Armenian, a tutor came to their house in Tehran. In the case of French, even though she did not attend the same French Lyceum as Nikit and Bella did, Emma from the age of seven traveled weekly to tutorial sessions with a French teacher. Her command of Farsi/Persian quickly developed at the local school near her home, which she attended from the age of seven. In addition to the priority given to language training, Emma also participated in weekly music and dance lessons. Having complained about piano lessons and scales, Emma was rather offered the opportunity to take accordion lessons from a Russian Armenian teacher who came weekly to the house. Her dance lessons began with a very accomplished Russian ballet dancer, Madame Cornelia, who ran a ballet school in Tehran, "Madame Cornelia's School of Ballet."

When Emma began attending the local all-girls Farsi school, she recalled having stomach cramps and discomfort because she had no friends. The teacher however took a liking to Emma, who was the tallest girl in her class, and asked Emma to assist by checking the other students each day for lice in their hair. When Emma's mother discovered that Emma too had contracted lice, she removed Emma from the school, and home-schooled Emma for a year—a year when Emma also contracted pleurisy at the age of eight. By age nine, Emma began attending an Armenian school, one of the Armenian schools that Emma's father was helping to support philanthropically. Most of her classes continued to be in Farsi, but the classes in Armenian language and history were taught out of Armenian. One of the problems Emma faced was that she did not really command Armenian, with the result that she was constantly needing to translate everything from Russian to Armenian to understand what was being read and discussed.

In the end, Emma felt she learned most from her Russian tutor, Mr. Bulgakov, even though she was able to communicate effectively also in Farsi by the time she began regular daily schooling. In effect, Emma continued to learn as much outside of her formal schooling in sessions with Bulgakov and her other tutors as she did in school. Her earliest work with English was probably during her play time with Maude, the neighboring daughter of an American Embassy foreign service officer. That exposure to English was supplemented by times when she would listen to an English tutor who played with her little niece Elsa. Toward the end of the family's time in Tehran, after plans were in place to emigrate to the United States, Emma worked intensively with an English tutor, Miss Mary, until the family's departure from Iran.

The Ordjanian Family Enterprise

In 1936, while Emma was still a toddler, her father managed to se-cure from Reza Shah Pahlavi's government a license to produce brandy and vodka in the northern Province of Mazandaran, the region of Iran im-mediately adjacent to the Caspian Sea. Such licenses required local Persian partnering, which brought the Ordjanian family into close collaboration with their Persian Iranian counterparts. The distillery and accompanying brewery, established in the Mazandaran provincial capital of Sari, became the largest of its kind in northern Iran, distributing beer as well as bran-dy, vodka, zubrovka, and fine wines. The beer bore the label of Four Stars Brewery. Adding to its regional distribution was the development of an on-sale retail site adjacent to the factory itself. So successful was the factory and its sales that Samson discontinued the chocolate manufacturing, giv-ing that over to his brother-in-law, Hashem Sherkat, the husband of Maria's sister Sonia. Emma noted that, at the height of its sales, the family beverage industry employed several hundred workers, including an army of women who oversaw the sterilization of returnable bottles.

Emma pictured here with some of the women in the foreground responsi-ble for bottling at the Ordjanian brewery in Sari (Mazandaran), Iran. Photo courtesy of the Ordjanian family.

Photo of a retail outlet selling alcohol produced at the Ordjanian distillery/brewery in the Mazandaran provincial capital of Sari. The photo taken during World War II is from a private album of Armen Elliott, provided here courtesy of the Ordjanian family.

Samson had to steer a careful line in heading an enterprise of alcohol production in a predominantly Islamic culture that effectively proscribed use of alcoholic beverages. Yet, as Emma later observed, it was not unusual for a Muslim woman to be seen "concealing purchase of a bottle in the folds of her chador" after having been dispatched to the retail store by a waiting husband or family member. The sensitivity of this intercultural exchange was dramatically apparent in an incident that left a profound impact on the Ordjanian family in 1938.

The incident occurred in one of the Mazandaran county seats, Qaem Shahr (known as Shahi prior to the 1979 Iranian Revolution). Shahi was a small city just southwest of the seacoast city of Babolsar, where the Ordjanian family would spend summers, and just west of the Mazandaran capital city of Sari, where the Ordjanian liquor enterprise had its main factory. In Shahi, Samson had rented the ground floor of the tallest building in the city center for retail sales and business offices. In 1938, government officials occupying other floors in the same building were apparently caught embezzling funds from Reza Shah's government. To cover their crime, the government officials set fire to the building. In his follow-on inquiry into the fire affecting his government's offices, Reza Shah Pahlavi asked the building's superintendent to identify the wealthiest tenant of the building. Learning that it was Samson Ordjanian, Reza Shah demanded Samson's arrest, no doubt finding it easier to pin the blame on a Persian-Armenian manufacturer of alcoholic beverages.

Samson was released on bail, but only after being forced to provide funds sufficient to rehabilitate the entire building. Nikit credits the ability of his father to secure such funding to Samson's sterling reputation within the wider Armenian community from whose members Samson was able to borrow the necessary funds. The 1938 incident documented both the vulnerability of minority Armenians in Persian society and, at the same time, the growing authority and prestige of the Ordjanian family name in interwar Iran. It was not until World War II that Samson was fully able to reimburse all his lenders.[8]

Ordjanian Support for Religious and Educational Institutions

The Ordjanian family became generous supporters of Armenian institutions in Iran, most notably seen in Samson's foundational support for an Armenian school in Sari, the city where the Ordjanian vodka distillery was situated. In addition, the family participated in and supported local Armenian church events, helping to fund St. George (Sorp Gevork) Armenian Church, one of the two oldest Armenian parishes in Tehran. Founded in the eighteenth century and still active today, the current St. George building in Tehran dates from 1882. There continue to be several functioning Armenian churches in Tehran, the oldest of them being the Armenian Apostolic Church of Saints Thaddeus and Bartholomew, which also was built in the eighteenth century.

---

8. Nikit Ordjanian, p. 29-30.

Armenian Apostolic Church of St. Gevork in Tehran
Photo from *https://en.wikipedia.org/wsiki/Saint_George_Church_of_Tehran,* ***accessed 4 March 2024.***

All the Armenian churches in Tehran in the interwar years were under the authority of the Armenian Catholicosate of Cilicia/Antelias—often referred to as churches of the prelacy—rather than diocesan churches under the authority of the Armenian Catholicos of Etchmiadzin. The split between Cilician and Etchmiadzin jurisdictions within the Armenian Apostolic Church was amplified in the interwar period by the anti-Communism of the Dashnaktsutyun Party (the Armenian Revolutionary Federation). Driven from the Caucasus region by the Bolsheviks, the Dashnaks saw the Catholicos of Etchmiadzin as somehow tainted by its association with the new Communist government in Soviet Armenia. The more nationalistic Dashnaks dominated the church politics of interwar Persian Armenians, whose churches remained under the authority of the Cilician Catholicosate. Samson and family, while they shared much of the anti-Communism of the Dashnaks, kept themselves at arms' length from the Cilician prelacy, attending the prelacy church of St. Gevork, but differentiating themselves from the more nationalistic Dashnak party leadership.

Summers

In the hottest months of the summer, the Ordjanian family typically abandoned Tehran for the cooler clime of the Mazandaran province and the Caspian Sea. They rented seaside housing in the resort town of Babolsar, and would also stay in their own two-story home attached to the liquor factory in the nearby Mazandaran capital of Sari. The rented house in Babolsar was regularly filled with visitors, often drawing families who could travel from Tehran to Babolsar by eight-hour train ride. Later, toward the end of their years in Iran, the family spent summer weeks at a seaside resort hotel in Ramsar where all meals were prepared for them (Ramsar is located further west on the Caspian southern shore—see the map above).

Emma (aged 12) at the Caspian Sea summer resort hotel in Ramsar at the close of World War II. Photo courtesy of the Melikian family archive.

The Ordjanians also maintained a second family home in Sari adjacent to the family liquor factory. The residence in Sari was on the second floor, with the ground floor used for retail sales and business offices. Each year, Emma's mother Maria would host a large dinner reception for the several hundred workers at the factory. Samson later purchased forty acres of property outside of Sari, and transferred the actual production facilities to the new location, but the two-story house in Sari remained for family and as a retail outlet.

The Coming of World War II

Into this relatively peaceful, harmonious setting, the dark clouds of what would become World War II loomed. Emma's birth in 1933 had followed by weeks the fall of the German Weimar government and Adolf Hitler's accession to power in the Third Reich. The autocratic Reza Shah Pahlavi was ever more conspicuously pro-German in his public pronouncements. Compounding the anxiety for the Ordjanians was the fact that their eldest son, Emma's brother Nikit, had left for Czechoslovakia in 1936, where he completed his baccalaureate degree on the eve of the outbreak of World War II, at which point his further studies in Czechoslovakia became impossible. Yet, Nazi ideologists considered Armenians and Iranians both to be "Aryan," with the result that, despite significant threats to his life with the onset of the war, Nikit was able to continue his studies in Freiburg during the war, completing his doctoral degree in 1944. By the time Nikit returned to Iran after the war—an absence of nine years—he had completed both his baccalaureate and doctoral degrees in mining engineering.

Emma's brother Nikit. Photo was taken in 1934 (age 16) when he was still a uniformed student at the Franco-Persan French Lyceum in Teheran, two years prior to his departure for higher education in Czechoslovakia and Germany. Photo is from the private album of Armen Elliot, and provided here courtesy of the Ordjanian family.

Meanwhile, the onset of war in Europe in 1939 and the subsequent collapse of the Nazi-Soviet Non-Aggression Pact in 1941 had dramatic impact on daily life in Tehran. Emma was just eight years old when, on August 25, 1941, under the code name Operation Countenance, joint British and Soviet allied armed forces invaded the nominally neutral Imperial State of Iran. The invasion came just two months after Germany had launched its invasion of the Soviet Union, at which point the USSR joined the alliance with the western Allies. The strategic significance of Iran for the Allies became that of maintaining a corridor for provisioning the Soviet Union and securing Iranian oil, including the Anglo-Persian oil fields and their Abadan refinery. Also driving the allied intervention was the concern over the pro-German sentiments of Reza Shah Pahlavi. His protection of German expatriates in Iran had become particularly troubling to the Allies.

Emma remembers the outbreak of the invasion on the morning of 25 August 1941, when a bomb landed within hearing distance in Tehran. She thought the bomb was delivered by Soviet forces, but it probably was dropped by a British bomber. Her memory of that day, however, was tied not just to the allied invasion of Iran, but also to the fact that on that very day, shortly after the bomb exploded, Emma's niece Elsa was born to Emma's sister Isabella. Bella had married Levon Karapetian, a handsome Russian Armenian émigré, in 1940. The birth of their first-born Elsa came on the same day, August 25, that the bomb exploded near Tehran marking the full-scale allied invasion of Iran.

Emma's older sister, Isabella, is pictured here in a wedding photo from 1940 when she married a fellow Persian-Armenian from Russia, Levon Karapetian in Tehran. The photo is from a private album of Armen Elliot, courtesy of the Ordjanian family.

More than 200,000 Allied forces, British and Soviet, converged on Iran, quickly overwhelming the limited resistance of Reza Shah Pahlavi's forces. The Shah had sought to modernize his army, but more for the purpose of controlling civilian population than for combatting powerful British and Soviet armies. Within four days, the Shah called for his troops to stand down. Iran was under full Allied occupation, an occupation that later would include 30,000 Americans. More than half of Iran, including Tehran and the northern Mazandaran province encompassing the Ordjanian liquor business holdings, came under Soviet military authority. Reza Shah was deposed in early September 1941, and his son Mohammed Pahlavi assumed the nominal title of Shah, but under Allied authority. To make it clear that this was not intended to be a long-term colonial occupation, both British and Soviet military generals pledged during the war that they would evacuate Iran within six months of the end of World War II, a goal that both powers kept, albeit with some delay from the Soviet Union, which had become deeply entrenched in northwestern Azerbaijan Iran.

Emma was just ten years old when the Allied powers, including Franklin Roosevelt, Winston Churchill, and Joseph Stalin, gathered in Tehran at the end of November 1943 for the Tehran Conference—the first time that Roosevelt met with the Soviet leader. Although there were several other Tehran Conference agreements, including the joint commitment to assist Iran and to guarantee Iranian independence after the war, the major outcome of the conference was the Allied agreement to Stalin's demand that a second front be established in Europe against the Germans, and that that front would be launched on the beaches of France by May 1944. One of the ironies of that outcome was that the Tehran Conference set in motion the set of events that would land Emma's future husband in France as a telegraph operator in the Supreme Allied Command headquarters outside Paris. At the time, however, young Emma was more attuned to the budding romance that she recalls between a lower echelon American translator traveling with the Roosevelt legation and a close female Persian-Armenian family acquaintance of the Ordjanians.

In contrast with the more general struggle for survival by many Iranians who faced food shortages and economic depression during the war, the Ordjanian liquor production business thrived. Serving the newly arrived Soviet Red Army forces in northern Iran alongside normal distribution, Samson's production and sale of vodka and zubrovka, as well as other fine wines and beer, soared in the years following Russian occupation of the Mazandaran province.[9] Indeed, as Emma recalls, it was this growth of the

---

9. While doing dissertation research in the Soviet Union in the late 1970s, I was privileged to meet and work with Iurii Efimovich Borshchevskii, the distinguished Iranist and head librarian of what was then the Leningrad Section of the Academy of Sciences' Institute of Oriental Studies (Leningradskii otdel, Institut vostokovedeniia). Borshchevskii spoke often about his service as an artillery officer and translator in northern Iran during World War II, remarking how fine the Armenian vodka and zubrovka were in that region. Borshchevskii was undoubtedly referring to products of the Ordjanian factory in Sari. For his obituary, see Stephen Batalden, *et al.*, "Iurii Efimovich Borshchevskii," *The Russian Review,* vol. 43, no. 1 (Jan. 1984), pp. 111-112.

business that made it possible for Samson to fund the family's subsequent emigration in 1948, two years after her brother Nikit paved the way with his own move to the United States. Samson was able to sell his business to his long-time Iranian accountant and partner, Anushavan, who joined other expert personnel in the distillery side of the business as they continued the enterprise after the Ordjanian departure. The sale of Ordjanian assets, including the liquor business and the two homes in Tehran and Sari, permitted the Ordjanians not only to fund the travel of Nikit and the extended Ordjanian family to the United States, but also to purchase for cash a home in Forest Hills, New York City, while also investing in rental properties purchased shortly after the family's safe arrival in America.

The years in Tehran were obviously formative for the young Emma. Her many tutors and extra-curricular lessons in music and dance more than substituted for her less rigorous formal schooling. Language study opened the world for Emma, as did the turbulent political climate in twentieth-century Iran. But, it was her extended family, often at the long table together, that nurtured her, protecting her in an atmosphere of love and generosity, sharing with her stories of earlier Communist persecution, and challenging her in the multi-cultural world of urban Tehran. It was also from her immediate family that she learned the significance of generosity and philanthropy, a philanthropy that included her father's launch of the Armenian school in the Mazandaran factory city of Sari. Not lost upon Emma was the transformative impact of the Ordjanians' financial commitment to Persian-Armenian schools and churches, a commitment that contributed significantly to the preservation and revitalization of the transplanted Armenian émigré community in interwar and wartime Iran.

3

America I – New York City

Emma Ordjanian was a Persian-Armenian during her formative years with family in Tehran and in Mazandaran, but while she remained a Persian-Armenian in her newly adopted country, she also became an American in her immigrant home of New York City. It was in New York where she became an American citizen, in New York where she received her advanced education, in New York where she married and began her own family, in New York where she was introduced to the complicated world of real estate and property ownership, and in New York where she committed herself and her family to a life of philanthropy.

All this began rather inauspiciously with the family's arrival in the United States in November 1948. Having spent a vacation week in Paris prior to their planned flight to New York, the party of six—Emma's mother Maria, her father Samson, her sister Isabella, her brother-in-law Levon Karapetian, her young niece Elsa, and Emma—arrived from France bearing gifts for everyone, including a set of attractive sheepskin coats for all the Ordjanian women, notably also for Nora (Eleanora Acopian), who just three months prior, in August 1948, had married Emma's brother Nikit. By the fall of 1948, two years after his own arrival in the U.S. (San Francisco), Nikit had not only married, but had also settled in New York after securing employment with MIDCO, the New York Mining and Industrial Company, with offices in Manhattan. Nikit had prepared for the family's arrival using funds advanced to him by his father to purchase a three-story home for the Ordjanians in the affluent Queens settlement of Forest Hills (71-19 Ingram Street). Despite Nikit's meticulous preparations, however, the actual arrival turned out to be rather disastrous.

Owing to bad weather, the Ordjanians' PanAm flight from Paris had to be diverted to Boston from its intended New York destination. Emma first set foot on American soil at Logan Airport in Boston. As she recounts, the women in their sheepskin coats disembarked onto the airport tarmac in a torrential downpour, the lovely coats ultimately taking on the unmistakable smell of wet sheep. Having tasked Emma with the role of primary translator, the family managed to connect with Nikit who helped arrange onward travel by train from Boston to New York City where they were at last reunited with Nikit and taken to their new home on Ingram Street in Forest Hills.

In purchasing the residence in Forest Hills, the Ordjanians were buying into an exclusive White Christian Anglo-Saxon (WASP) enclave that only a few years before would have been foreclosed to them. Forest Hills, Forest Hills Gardens, Kew Gardens, and the Forest Hills West Side Tennis Club had been for most of the period prior to World War II governed by written and unwritten restrictive covenants that specifically forbade African-American, Jewish, and other non-WASP immigrant groups from membership and residency. Unlike the even more restrictive Forest Hills Gardens, Forest Hills proper had been open to Armenian, Jewish, and other ethnic/religious minorities since World War II. Nevertheless, the distinguished African-American U.N. and U.S. diplomat Ralph Bunche, who purchased a residence in Forest Hills not far from the Ordjanian residence in 1950 (using proceeds from his Nobel Peace Prize earnings to do so), was denied membership for his son in the West Side Forest Hills Tennis Club explicitly on the grounds that "membership was not open to Negroes and Jews."[1] Like the Bunche family, the Ordjanians became part of the opening of Forest Hills, and the gradual elimination there of restrictive covenants.

---

1. This was the explicit language used by Club President Wilfred Burglund, a Manhattan public relations executive, who said that the Tennis Club (where the U.S. Open Tournament is played) could not admit Ralph Bunche, Jr., because it did not admit Negroes or Jews. When this exclusionary policy became known, a firestorm erupted, including a sharply worded statement issued by former first lady Eleanor Roosevelt. In the end, Burglund was forced to resign from the presidency of the Forest Hill Tennis Club, and the governors notified Bunche that the Club would give "courteous and prompt attention" to a membership bid on behalf of Dr. Bunche. Hearing this, Bunche replied that, under the circumstances, it was unlikely that he would be resubmitting his application for membership. See "Forest Hills Invites Bunche Application; Head of Club Quits," *New York Times*, July 15, 1959, p. 1, 12.

71-19 Ingram Street, Forest Hills [2]

Fifteen-year-old Emma faced comparable immigrant barriers in terms of her schooling. To overcome any lingering problems she might encounter with English, the family initially enrolled Emma in English tutorial training at Kew-Forest School, an exclusive private institution in Forest Hills. (Kew-Forest was the grammar school attended by Donald Trump prior to his removal to a military academy outside New York City.[3]) Emma recalls how her English improved under the tutelage of "Mrs. Smith."

---

2. Photo is edited from Google Maps (https://www.google.com/maps/@40.714362,-73.8476353,3a,75y,41.34h,90t/data=!3m7!1e1!3m5!1soYWc0O8Rh9dOzv1W6J_UY-Q!2e0!6shttps:%2F%2Fstreetviewpixels-pa.googleapis.com%2Fv1%2Fthumbnail%3F-panoid%3DoYWc0O8Rh9dOzv1W6J_UYQ%26cb_client%3Dsearch.gws-prod.gps%26w%3D86%26h%3D86%26yaw%3D41.336674%26pitch%3D0%26thumbfo-v%3D100!7i16384!8i8192?entry=ttu), last accessed on 2/11/2024.

3. The claim that Donald Trump was expelled from Kew-Forest School for slapping his teacher is unconfirmed. The more common explanation for Trump's removal from Kew-Forest School at the end of seventh grade was that of his father's anger over the discovery of his son's knives and unauthorized travel with male classmates on the subway into Manhattan. In 2016, the *Washington Post* interviewed several of Trump's classmates and teachers from Kew-Forest School and the New York Military Academy where his father transferred him after the seventh grade. Although his classmates and teachers all remember him for his surly, bullying character, they do not confirm the account that he was expelled from Kew-Forest School for slapping one of his teachers. Whether out of concern for reprisals or from honest recollection, the teacher in question, Charles Walker, denies having been slapped by Donald, although he did not speak kindly about the young Kew-Forest mischief maker. See Paul Schwartzman and Michael Miller, "Confident. Incorrigible. Bully: Little Donny Was a Lot Like Candidate Donald Trump," *Washington Post,* June 22, 2016. See also Michael Kranish and Marc Fisher, *Trump Revealed: An American Journey of Ambition, Ego, Money, and Power* (New York: Scribner, 2016).

Kew-Forest School, Forest Hills, NYC (from <u>https://foresthillstimes.</u>
<u>com/2018/10/14/kew-forest-school-open-house/</u>***, accessed 3/4/2024)***

The tutoring lasted only two months during the late fall of 1948 before Emma, for financial reasons, was transferred to the local public high school, Forest Hills High School. Unprepared to work with a newly arrived immigrant with uncertain English skills, Forest Hills High School authorized Emma to attend a variety of classes, but without official registration for any of them. This pattern persisted into the spring of 1949 when the school hosted the visit of the New York superintendent of schools, along with members of the local school board. One of the purposes of the site visit was to determine the appropriateness of incorporating immigrant English learners like Emma Ordjanian into Forest Hills High School. For the occasion, Emma was asked to give an oral presentation for the visiting delegation in one of the Forest Hills High School speech classes. The quality of her presentation in English was apparently so polished that the delegation was confounded. Why was this student being kept at arm's length from regularly registered classes? From that point onward Emma was mainstreamed into regular freshman classes at Forest Hills High School, graduating with several hundred classmates three years later in the spring of 1952.

Nevertheless, the relative unpreparedness of Forest Hills High School in addressing the needs of a bright, inquisitive immigrant teenager from the Middle East is a part of the wider story of the post-World War II integration/desegregation of the Forest Hills enclave. Today that integration has come full circle. Forest Hills High School is an institution with more than 3,600 students in grades 9-12. The school boasts a student population with 75% minority enrollment, including 6.2% African-American; 39.5%

Forest Hills High School (photo taken from school website,
https://www.foresthillshs.org/)

Hispanic, and 25.2% Asian-American.[4] Emma Ordjanian might have difficulty recognizing the school she attended.

As in Tehran, so also in New York, Emma's schooling extended well beyond the formal classroom. Weekly dance lessons were held in Manhattan under the tutelage of an elderly associate of the late Russian choreographer and ballet innovator, Michel Fokine (1880-1942). Her voice lessons, also arranged weekly in Manhattan, were with a Russian teacher who had earlier worked with the great Russian opera star, Feodor Chaliapin (1873-1938). In addition, Emma joined the young people's photography club sponsored by the New York chapter of the Armenian General Benevolent Union (AGBU). These co-curricular lessons and group activities not only broadened the scope of Emma's training, but brought her into regular contact with Armenian- and Russian-speaking young people of her own generation. The considerable skills she developed also enriched her adult years, notably as a gifted singer serving in church choirs into her seventies, and as an amateur photographer recording her extensive international travels later in life.

Alongside these diverse curricular and co-curricular programs of study, Emma was enlisted as a translator and assistant for major projects launched

---

4. For the current ethnic composition of Forest Hills High School, see the *U.S. News & World Report* ranking profile on their website: https://www.usnews.com/education/best-high-schools/new-york/districts/new-york-city-public-schools/forest-hills-high-school-13358, last accessed 9/10/2023.

by her father and mother. In the case of her father Samson, who began to invest in New York rental property shortly after arriving in America, Emma would routinely accompany her father, serving as translator when her father met with real estate agents, bankers, property owners, and tenants. She noted that her father spoke Russian, Farsi, and Armenian, but was not fluent in English. "I became his tongue," she commented. It was during those sessions that Emma began to command the subtleties of down payments, mortgages, interest, the New York City rent control system, and all manner of tenant requests and complaints. In addition to their home in Forest Hills, Samson ultimately purchased and managed four apartment buildings in Manhattan and Queens, each with twenty rental units. When Emma later met her future husband, the young lawyer Gregory Melikian who shared interests in property investment and rental management, she was already a formidable partner and authority in her own right on New York City rental property.

Similarly, when Emma's mother Maria began to teach the Armenian language and traditional songs to Armenian-American children in Forest Hills in small weekend classes arranged in people's homes, Emma was her assistant. Maria also helped spearhead each year an evening of dinner and dance sponsored by the Iranian Armenian Society, where Emma would perform. It was at one such Armenian-American gathering of Maria's students and their parents held in the spring of 1953 in the rented facilities of Forest Hills Inn in the Gardens, that Gregory Melikian first set eyes on Emma who was again that evening performing an Armenian dance number at the event organized by her mother.

Emma's graduation from Forest Hills High School in the spring of 1952 (see graduation photo below provided courtesy of Melikian Family Archive) was the natural culmination of these formative, engaging years in America. To mark her graduation Samson and Maria purchased for Emma her first car, a dark blue 1952 Buick sedan. The one condition that Samson attached to the purchase was that Emma would have to serve as the driver for a summer tour across the United States—a trip on which Samson, who never secured an American driver's license and never drove a car, would gladly accompany Emma. Throughout the early summer of 1952, Emma, her mother, father, and brother-in-law Levon Karapetian (Emma's sister Isabella, having recently given birth to a second daughter Mary, remained in New York) traveled across the Midwest to the West Coast and through California before returning via Arizona, the Grand Canyon, and the American southwest.

Announcement of 3ʳᵈ Annual Iranian Armenian Society Dinner and Dance, May 19, 1951, featuring in the center picture Emma Ordjanian performing a "Caucasian Dance." Announcement is preserved in and provided courtesy of the Melikian Family Archive. Emma's high school graduation photo is on right.

A model of a blue 1952 Buick Sedan, Emma's first car

Those were happy days for Emma and her parents. Emma recalls how her father was particularly impressed with the well-kept farms and small towns of the American Midwest. For someone who had experienced the poverty of rural Russia and of Iran, including the dramatic difference in living standards between urban and rural life on the Eurasian steppe, the tidy, clean, modern towns of the Midwest made an unmistakable impression on Samson. Emma recounts how, as they passed by small towns and immaculate, freshly-painted farmhouses, Samson would repeatedly proclaim in his heavily accented-English, "What a country! What a country!"

Samson and all the Ordjanians were admirers of Gen. Eisenhower, and remained loyal Republicans throughout the 1950s, even though they had yet to be naturalized as citizens and were unable to vote in the 1952 election. Her brother Nikit was also a loyal Eisenhower supporter and would remain a Republican to his death in 2004. Emma, who shared her family's political sentiments, nevertheless broke with her Republican loyalties in opposition to the presidency of Donald Trump. As she notes, "I did not abandon the Republican Party; the Republican Party abandoned me."

During the fall 1952 election cycle Emma began her higher education at an innovative junior college launched in 1946 through the New York City YMCA. This "Y school," as it was called, constituted an early introduction into New York City of the kind of junior college vocational and commercial training for men and women that became increasingly popular in the second half of the twentieth century. Named for a member of the managing board of the YMCA schools and a long-time assistant superintendent of schools in New York, Dr. Walter L. Hervey, the Walter Hervey Junior College was located within the West Side YMCA on 63rd Street in Manhattan, where Emma began her program with a major in industrial psychology. As was noted by the *New York Times* on the occasion of its establishment in 1946, the plan for this experiment in cooperative education—the first of its kind in the state—was to provide for twelve-week semesters of study to be followed by twelve-week internships in which students would engage in full-time business activity related to their course of study.[5] The original curriculum offered two-year degrees in business administration and related fields. The student body was initially limited to two hundred students to be competitively admitted, and taught by fifteen faculty members. By the time Emma entered, in 1952, the major in industrial psychology that she pursued had been added to the cur-

---

5. "Cooperative College to be Run by Y.M.C.A.," *New York Times,* April 5, 1946, p. 25.

riculum. In addition to general liberal arts courses, her major focused
on labor-management relations. The
tuition was $150 per year. Emma re-
calls the special attention she received
from Walter Hervey faculty members, one of whom even coached her,
shy as she was at the time, on self-presentation for an American corporate
culture. Although she participated in
the June 1953 Walter Hervey Junior
College Commencement (bulletin
for which is attached here courtesy
of the Melikian family archive), she is
listed as graduating with the class of
September 1953.[6]

It was while attending Walter
Hervey College that Emma first met
Gregory Melikian. After having seen

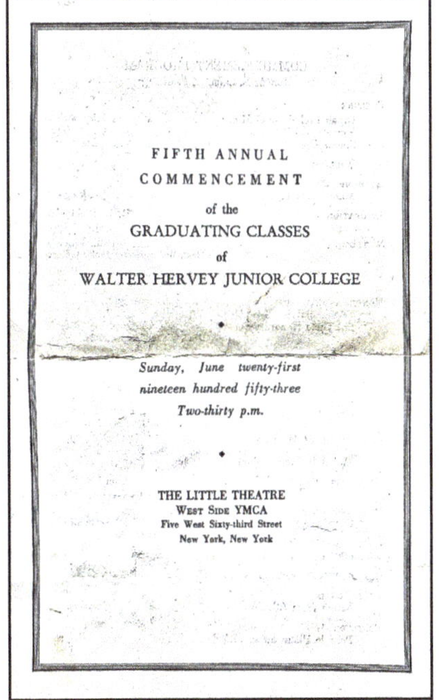

Emma dancing at the 1953 gala spring gathering of Armenian-Americans
in Forest Hills Inn, Gregory contacted Emma's brother Nikit, and through
him managed to secure Emma's telephone number. Emma recalls a lengthy
hour-long first conversation with Gregory by phone that surprised her
by the many interests they shared, including their interest in international affairs, international travel, real estate, and property management. The
ensuing courtship included extended rides home that Gregory offered to
Emma, picking her up on evenings after her classes at Walter Hervey Junior College.

The attractive young college student and recently-minted New York
lawyer became engaged following Emma's graduation from Walter Hervey,
Gregory having secured the necessary approval of Emma's father Samson.
The wedding on 12 June 1954, was held in the cathedral church of the Ar-
menian prelacy (the Cilician Armenian Catholicosate), St. Illuminator's
Armenian Apostolic Cathedral on 27th Street in Manhattan. St. Illumina-

---

6. "Fifth Annual Commencement of the Graduating Classes of Walter Hervey Junior
College, Sunday, June 21, 1953, 2:30 p.m., The Little Theatre, West Side YMCA, 5 West 63rd
Street, New York, NY." Pictured bulletin is copied here from the original preserved in the
Melikian Family Archive.

tor referenced St. Gregory the Illuminator, the fourth-century founder of the Armenian Apostolic Church, for whom many an Armenian "Gregory" has been named, including Gregory Melikian.

Although family members outside the United States were unable to attend, the marriage of Gregory and Emma brought together the large extended Ordjanian family (including Rustamian relatives who remained in Iran and the Soviet Union) and the much smaller Melikian family, including Gregory's mother, Armenouhi, a survivor of the Armenian genocide in World War I.

Wedding photo of Ordjanian and Melikian families. From left standing: Nikit & Nora Ordjanian; Levon Karapetian; Gregory and Emma Melikian; Samson Ordjanian; and Isabella Karapetian. lower level from left: Maria Ordjanian; Armenouhi Melikian; and Elsa Karapetian.

Gregory's father, who ran his own trucking company in New York, had died suddenly overseas while on a 1953 vacation travel that reconnected Gregory's parents with a surviving sister of Armenouhi. The sister, Yester, had married an Armenian accountant who worked for a Turkish shipping company in Istanbul. As survivors of the Armenian genocide, Gregory's mother and grandmother had found refuge in Bulgaria where Gregory's mother was sheltered by Catholic nuns in a local orphanage. One of the side consequences of Armenouhi's Catholic upbringing was that, following emigration to New York in 1923, she married Gregory's father Hagop in a Catholic church in greater New York, and Gregory would later be baptized in the Catholic church. Nonetheless, the Ordjanian-Melikian marriage was in the Armenian Apostolic Church, and their family would be raised in the Armenian church.

The Ordjanian-Melikian marriage was a lavish affair, with guests hosted following the ceremony at the Russian restaurant Balalaika, adjoining the well-known Russian Tea Room in Manhattan. Emma's bridal party included Janet Karolian (maid of honor and dance school friend whose uncle and aunt were the best man/maid of honor for the wedding of Nikit and Nora Ordjanian) and Seda Sahakian (a close family acquaintance at Walter Hervey College), as well as the younger flower girls, Emma's niece Elsa and cousin Joyce Shushan [later Barsam]).

Emma and Gregory departed for a honeymoon in Bermuda, traveling there by ocean cruise liner, and returning to New York by air. Following an initial home in Queens that ended up being rather unpleasant overlooking a cemetery, the newly married couple moved to an apartment they rented in Kew Garden Hills (70-01 Park Drive East).

70-01 Park Drive East, Kew Garden Hills, New York City [7]

The first year of married life was particularly daunting for Emma. She faced two moves, ultimately settling into the comfortable one-bedroom apartment in Kew Garden Hills. She applied for and received naturaliza-

---

7. Google Maps (2024). Available at https://www.google.com/maps/place/7001+Park+Dr+E,+Flushing,+NY+11367/@40.7267873,-73.8308924,3a,75y,73.93h,90t/data=!3m7!1e1!3m5!1sG-57nVJffVUYla2u-MfG0g!2e0!6shttps:%2F%2Fstreetview-pixels-pa.googleapis.com%2Fv1%2Fthumbnail%3Fpanoid%3DG-57nVJffVUYla2u-Mf-G0g%26cb_client%3Dsearch.gws-prod.gps%26w%3D360%26h%3D120%26yaw%3D73.93%26pitch%3D0%26thumbfov%3D100!7i16384!8i8192!4m15!1m8!3m7!1s0x89c-260858c0229b3:0x8a714bdebb9916b9!2s7001+Park+Dr+E,+Flushing,+NY+11367!3b1!8m2!3d40.7268225!4d-73.8307049!16s%2Fg%2F11hf14bqq0!3m5!1s0x89c260858c0229b3:0x8a714bdebb9916b9!8m2!3d40.7268225!4d-73.8307049!16s%2Fg%2F11hf14bqq0?entry=ttu, accessed 6 March 2024.

tion as a U.S. citizen on November 11, 1954. She was admitted into Barnard College, a prominent women's institution affiliated with Columbia University where she began a one-year night-school program for returning adult students focused on architectural and interior design. That program today is part of the Barnard College Design Center (https://design.barnard.edu/) that offers the B.S. degree in design and postgraduate programs, alongside the adult training programs in which Emma was enrolled. While at Barnard, she also began assisting Gregory with property management and some remodeling efforts—tasks she was still also performing for her father Samson.

U.S., Naturalization Records Indexes, 1794-1995
New York > Eastern District of New York > McGaffin, Hugh to Melluzzo, Sabastiano

No. 7387434

Name MELIKIAN Emma

residing at 70-01 Park Drive East, Kew Garden Hills, NY

Date of birth April 4, 1933 Date of order of admission Nov. 11, 1954

Date certificate issued Nov. 11, 1954 by the

U. S. District Court at Brooklyn, New York

Petition No. 517411

Alien Registration No. 7. __ 7.841

(Complete and true signature of holder)

Emma Ordjanian Melikian's official naturalization document [8]

In that same first year of marriage when she began her Barnard program in interior design, Emma faced the unexpected death of her father who succumbed to a third heart attack and died in early February 1955. He had been weakened by prior heart attacks, forcing the move of her parents from their Ingram Street three-story home to a single-floor apartment unit. His death was a huge loss for Emma and the entire extended Ordjanian family.

The passing of Samson Ordjanian marked the end of an era—one which had seen the rise of the Ordjanian family, lifted as they were by the indefatigable enterprising energy of a businessman who managed to carve

8. National Archives and Records Administration, Wash., D. C. *Index to Naturalization Petitions in the United States District Court for the Eastern District of New York, 1865-1957.* Microfilm Serial: M1164; Microfilm Roll 93 (accessed through Ancestry.com. U.S. Naturalization Records Indexes, 1794-1995. Lehi, UT, 2007).

out a successful career in unimaginably complicated Russian and Iranian environments. The sad irony of his passing was that declining health had cut short his life just when the external impediments to his entrepreneurship had vanished. Emma's brother Nikit recalls an emotional moment when, after arranging for his father to receive social security, he brought Samson his first FICA check in January 1955, shortly before his passing. According to Nikit, Samson remarked:

> What a country! I lived many years in Russia and contributed to that country by creating jobs for hundreds of Russians. My eventual reward was jail and loss of all my possessions. I lived many years in Iran where I likewise created jobs for many Iranians, the Shah arbitrarily put me into jail and ruined me financially. I came to the United States too late in my life to make a meaningful contribution here, but the government provides me now with a monthly check for life. God bless America.[9]

Nikit added that it was the first time he had seen tears in his father's eyes. As patriarch of the Ordjanian family, Samson had been a loving father who had been deeply supportive of his younger daughter Emma.

Offsetting the grief of her father's passing, Emma had become pregnant and her firstborn son, James, was born on 23 July 1955. But even James's birth ended up being rather traumatic, following as it did an unusually extended three-day period of labor. From citizenship to baccalaureate studies to her father's passing and James's birth, the 21-year-old Emma's first year of marriage was marked by hard work, profound sadness, and immense joy.

Emma's new U.S. citizenship, the loss of her father, her promising academic studies, and her marriage to Gregory Melikian all served to sharpen her transition from Persian-Armenian daughter to independent American homemaker and professional woman. It was not that her roots in the Russian-Armenian and Persian-Armenian communities were abandoned. She maintained close family ties, held onto her spoken Russian, and nurtured her young family in Armenian traditions. But, alongside those continuities with the past, Emma was building with Gregory a family future grounded in wise and frugal property investment, civic engagement, and generous philanthropy. The transition was perhaps most clear in the disposal of her

---

9. Nikit Ordjanian, "To Anahid and Armen with Love," p. 67.

father's property following his death. Emma's brother Nikit arranged for the sale of the rental properties owned by Samson, freeing Emma to assist Gregory in the development of what would be their own substantial property holdings in New York City. The assets from the sale of the Ordjanian properties were invested in AT&T stock, monthly earnings from which permitted Emma's mother Maria to lead a comfortable lifestyle, including two separate journeys back to Iran and the Soviet Union in the 1950s for visits with close Rustamian family relatives.

Fifteen years lay between Emma's marriage to Gregory and the migration of the family westward to Arizona in 1969. During those fifteen years Emma's life in New York City came to revolve around her growing family, her support for the family's successful real estate ventures, her civic engagements, and the increasingly generous philanthropic commitments she launched with Gregory's support. With respect to family, Emma oversaw a large team of support for the growing Melikian offspring. That team included two widowed grandmothers (Maria and Armenouhi), and a host of more extended Ordjanian and Melikian family members. Gloria Shushan (later, Hachikian), a second cousin on Gregory's side of the family who would occasionally spend weeks in the summer at the Melikian home later acquired in Kew Gardens, recalls how well-organized Emma was. Even in the moments of her private space, Emma kept to a rigorous routine, with attention to good grooming and self-presentation—matters the young Gloria (later a dealer in designer clothing) followed closely. When a second child, Robert (b. 6 September 1956), was born little more than a year after James's birth, Emma would ultimately hire two live-in assistants, the Armenian sisters Hermina and Sakah, to care for the young toddlers. To house the growing family, to accommodate multiple visits from relatives, and later to house the Armenian nannies required space well beyond that of the Melikians' one-bedroom apartment in Kew Garden Hills.

The answer to the space problem came in the form of one of Gregory's legendary property acquisitions—the three-story, 4,000 square foot mansion at 84-62 Beverly Road in Kew Gardens. According to legend, and reconfirmed by Emma, Gregory had heard of the likely future sale of the Beverly Road home by its owners who were going through contested divorce proceedings. As he would do on other occasions, Gregory decided to go directly with Emma to the source, knocking on the door of the house and offering to purchase it from the owners. Although their overture was

84-62 Beverly Road in Kew Gardens
Photo courtesy of Melikian Family Archive.

initially rejected by the female owner who shut the door on them, considering Gregory and Emma far too young to be able to afford such a house, they did not give up. The young couple returned to the house after learning that, by then, the divorced wife whom they had earlier met had inherited the property in the divorce settlement, and was preparing to sell it. In the end, Gregory's offer to pay cash for the property, allowing the homeowner also to avoid real estate fees, sealed the deal, and the Melikians became owners of an unusual Japanese pagoda-style mansion in one of the finer sections adjoining Forest Hills.[10]

Purchase of the Beverly Road property also drew Emma more deeply into Melikian property management because she assumed responsibility for the remodeling and interior design of additional rooms in a previously unfinished basement level, effectively increasing by 25 percent the square footage of the building. Emma's entry into property remodeling and interi-

10. For a good recounting of the purchase of the Beverly Road property, see the biography of Gregory Melikian by Lee B. Croft, *Peace and Preservation: The Life of Gregory Melikian* (Phoenix: Sphynx Publications, 2023), 198-202.

or design, while it may have come quite naturally to her, also had been advanced by her night-school academic program at Barnard College. Emma would never complete the Barnard degree and interior design licensing program, which required a full-time internship incompatible with her new role as homemaker and remodeling designer, but she credits the program for training her in interior design and also for introducing her to fellow students who would later become points of linkage to civic institutions she came to support, including the New York Metropolitan Opera Guild.

The Beverly Road property also had the advantage of its location within four blocks of Public School 99 (P.S.99), which all three Melikian sons attended, including third son Richard (b. 1 March 1958). Even daughter Ramona reached kindergarten age and attended P.S. 99 prior to the family's move to Phoenix. James would set the example, joining a gifted program at P.S. 99. James's class was privileged to share a linkage with the Brooklyn Museum, traveling there Saturdays with close friends to set up treasure hunts at the Egyptian Pavilion for visiting students coming to the Museum on weekends. Robert would receive a JFK medal of honor for the most popular child in the school. Richard, in addition to being a good student, was active in sports events at the school. The Melikian children were well grounded, and P.S. 99 offered the advantages of solid primary school training in a convenient, secure upscale neighborhood setting.

***Public School 99, Kew Gardens (Photo from** https://www.flickr.com/
photos/mateox/14085850344/in/photostream/**)***

The birth of Ramona, while it completed the immediate Melikian family, was also accompanied by nostalgic memories for Emma of her own family's distant past. In a strange coincidence, the Armenian priest, Father Artem Simonian, who had married Emma's father and mother in Moscow in 1917, and then, as an émigré Armenian cleric in New York City, also married Emma and Gregory, baptized Ramona in 1963.

While Emma was consumed with raising her family, her work at Barnard had reopened access to a cultural world in New York that held significant importance for her, and later also for Gregory. From her earliest years in Tehran, Emma learned to appreciate opera, guided by her brother Ashot, who loved opera and listened

Melikian children from left: Richard, James, Ramona, and Robert. Photo from 1967 is courtesy of the Melikian Family Archive.

often to opera on recordings. In New York, she joined family members attending performances at the "Old Met," the famous Metropolitan Opera House with a seating capacity of close to four thousand, located on Broadway Avenue between 39th and 40th Streets. The Metropolitan Opera would continue to perform there until 1966, when it moved into the new Metropolitan Opera House located in Lincoln Center. While attending the year-long program on architectural and interior design at Barnard, Emma joined one of her classmates in occasional outings to architectural sites, including the Lincoln Center then under construction. It was also at this time that Emma joined the Metropolitan Opera Guild, becoming one of its more active contributing members.[11] Emma's attraction to the Metropolitan Opera grew out of her training in high culture, and her devotion to opera and ballet in particular—a devotion that was common among Russian

---

11. On the Metropolitan Opera Guild, which continues to be active, see its website, https://www.metguild.org/.

and East European intelligentsia as well as the population-at-large in Eastern Europe and Eurasia.[12] Emma recounts that she took Robert with her to "Live from Lincoln Center" performances, adding that "the kids knew that opera was a part of my life." On Saturday, Emma would regularly listen to the Metropolian Opera matinee performances on radio.

Emma's philanthropy during her years in New York City extended well beyond opera and the arts. Emma and Gregory became visible leaders and contributors also within the Armenian-American community. In 1954, the newly-married couple was invited to join twelve other couples in a building committee for a new Armenian church to be constructed on Long Island. The first meeting of the committee, held when Emma was pregnant with James, was the occasion also for meeting Father Torkom Manoogian, a talented young cleric and translator of Shakespearean sonnets into Armenian who was then serving an Armenian diocesan parish in north Philadelphia. Father Torkom would serve as the facilitator of the effort to build the new Armenian diocesan parish on Long Island.

Torkom Manoogian (1919-2012) [13]

12. The national and international significance of opera was dramatically in evidence more recently in the immediate aftermath of the Russian military invasion of Ukraine when the Metropolitan Opera's general manager Peter Gelb announced on 28 February 2022 that owing to the war in Ukraine the Met would sever all ties with performers, staff, and employees who supported Russian President Vladimir Putin. That same evening, prior to the premiere performance of Verdi's *Don Carlos,* the Met's orchestra and chorus performed for a sold-out standing audience the "State Anthem of Ukraine." Center stage making his debut performance with the Met that evening was the Ukrainian bass-baritone soloist, Vladyslav Buialski, the only performer singing the anthem without a score. The performance aired to riveted audiences on outlets broadcasting throughout Ukraine. See Javier C. Hernandez, "On a Stage 5,000 Miles Away, He Sings for His Family in Ukraine, *The New York Times,* March 13, 2022 (https://www.nytimes.com/2022/03/13/arts/music/met-opera-ukraine-russia.html, last accessed on 19 September 2023). For the performance of the anthem, listen to https://www. gramophone.co.uk/classical-music-news/article/video-of-the-day-met-opera-performs-ukrainian-national-anthem, last accessed on 19 September 2023.
13. Photo is from *HyeTert,* a journal of the United States' eastern diocese of the Armenian Apostolic Church (from https://hyetert.org/2014/01/24/celebrate-the-legacy-of-archbish-op-manoogian/, accessed 4 March 2024).

The division of the Armenian church into "diocesan" and "prelacy" parishes had its distant origins in the fifteenth century when the old center of Armenian population in the Kingdom of Cilicia (southern Anatolia) was operating with its own independent church head, the Catholicos of Cilicia. During the fifteenth century, it became possible to reestablish the original catholicosate in Etchmiadzin (the location just outside Yerevan) where the Armenian Catholicos resides today. But there remained the two catholicosates into the twentieth century, with the Cilician Catholicos residing in Antelias, Lebanon, and the Etchmiadzin Catholicos residing in Armenia. In the United States the relationship between the Cilician Catholicosate with its "prelacy" parishes and the Etchmiadzin Catholicosate with its "diocesan" parishes became embittered by fractious Cold War differences. Those differences came to a dramatic climax following the appointment in 1931 of Leon Tourian as primate (head) of the eastern diocese of the Armenian Apostolic Church (under the Etchmiadzin Catholicosate). Tourian was particularly cautious of his position amidst the diaspora and its relationship to an Etchmiadzin-based Armenian church that found itself under Soviet oppression.

In July 1933, while visiting "Armenian Day" at the "Century of Progress Exposition in Chicago," Archbishop Tourian asked that the red, blue, and orange tricolor flag of the first Republic of Armenia (1918-20, the tricolor is also the flag of today's Republic of Armenia) be removed from the podium prior to his delivery of the invocation. Tourian obviously feared how the presence of the flag might be interpreted back in Soviet Armenia. The incident was not lost upon diaspora adherents of the rival Cilician prelacy parishes, strongly supported as they were by former members of the nationalist Armenian Dashnak Party (Armenian Revolutionary Federation, founded in 1890). The flag incident fed the fears of such Armenian Dashnak nationalists that the Etchmiadzin parishes were compromised by being under the sway of Soviet Communist authorities. This division within ethnic churches of the diaspora between those loyal to the authority of traditional homeland church hierarchy (albeit a church under Communist rule) and those nationalists loyal to alternative church authority has plagued many other East European diaspora communities, including the Russian and Serbian churches of the emigration.

The division within the Armenian church in America came to a head in 1933 when, at the high Armenian liturgical service of Christmas Eve,

Archbishop Tourian was assassinated during the opening procession of clergy at the diocesan Armenian Church of the Holy Cross in Manhattan.[14] New York authorities ultimately apprehended the nine perpetrators, all members of the nationalist ARF (Dashnaks). Two were subsequently convicted of murder, the remaining seven convicted of first-degree manslaughter. The legacy of the Christmas Eve assassination lived on in the continuing split within the Armenian church of the diaspora.

From his days in Iran, Samson and the Ordjanian family had worshipped in prelacy parishes where Dashnaks prevailed, but he never identified himself with the Dashnak nationalist revolutionaries. While Ordjanians and Rustamians would occasionally worship in prelacy parishes, and Emma and Gregory were married in the New York cathedral church of the prelacy, Emma, despite her anti-Communism, nevertheless recognized the authority of the Etchmiadzin Catholicos and was prepared to support the building of the Long Island diocesan church. The neutrality of the Melikian family in this church split may be seen in the fact that, while support followed for the building of the church on Long Island, the Melikian children were nevertheless all baptized by the aging Father Simonian in prelacy parishes.

When the Long Island building committee was formed, and Father Torkom began men's and womens' associations for the church, Emma was receptive to this overture. Gregory was also supportive, linking his name and the Melikian family with twelve other up-and-coming young couples from the Armenian-American community of New York on a building committee for what would be called the Armenian Apostolic Church of the Holy Martyrs. Land for the parish was donated by three members of the original building committee—Artin Aslanian, Dadour Dadourian, and Poozant Piranian.

The leadership of Torkom Manoogian in this effort was also critical. Father Torkom was a revered parish priest in the diocesan church, but also a scholar and poet in his own right. Born in Baghdad and trained at the Jerusalem Seminary of the Armenian Apostolic Church, Father Torkom was consecrated bishop, serving from 1966 to 1990 as primate of the eastern diocese of the Armenian Church in America—the position once held by the assassinated prelate Leon Tourian. Archbishop Torkom, who was later awarded an honorary doctorate by General Theological Seminary in Manhattan, was a distinguished ecumenist, a board member of the U.S. National Council of Churches, and a good friend of the Melikians. When

---

14. "Archbishop Assassinated in Procession to Altar," *New York Times*, 25 December 1933, p. 1.

the Melikian family later moved to Arizona, Archbishop Torkom would come to visit donors in Arizona, residing with the Melikians and spending short vacation periods of rest at the Melikian home in the Arcadia district of Phoenix. Later, Archbishop Torkum helped to inspire the founding of the Armenian diocesan church in Scottsdale, Arizona.

The building of the Church of the Holy Martyrs on Long Island was completed and formally dedicated in 1958. The naming of the church—Holy Martyrs—was one commonly used for new Armenian parishes in the diaspora, referencing those who perished in the 1915 Armenian Genocide during World War I. The Melikian family became charter members of the parish.

That Emma and Gregory were able to contribute generously to such philanthropic and community efforts owed largely to their success in investment and management of residential rental property in New York. The Melikian enterprise ultimately amounted to eight apartment buildings across the city, in addition to their large Beverly Road home. In all, more than two hundred rental units came under the ownership and management of the Melikians, two and a half times the size of the holdings amassed earlier by Emma's father Samson.[15]

Armenian Apostolic Church of the Holy Martyrs
209-15 Harding Expressway, Bayside, NY [16]

15. The figures, confirmed by Emma, are taken from the Gregory Melikian biography by Lee Croft, *Peace and Preservation,* op. cit., p. 206.
16. https://www.google.com/maps/place/Armenian+Church+of+the+Holy+Martyrs/@40.7463542,-73.7679734,3a,75y,103.43h,90t/data=!3m7!1e1!3m5!1sAABDoSmsxyCD-

All eight apartment buildings came under New York City's rent control regime. What the rent control system meant was that profits from rental of such units, while they might be gained from normally inflated values at the time of sale, were strictly limited and controlled while the properties were held. The result was that owners, including the Melikians, needed to monitor closely the costs of improvements since increases in rent were strictly limited. As Emma has noted, since Gregory initially had only one secretarial assistant in his law offices, Emma was invariably the one who ended up responding to tenant complaints. She indicated,

> I was the one who had to respond to tenants, I checked with the tenants to determine when painting was needed, listened to complaints, and even went to court to respond to their complaints. If there were even one or two violations, the tenants' union could try to justify paying a simple $1/month rent. Gregory's secretary Tina remained in the office, but I had to deal with tenants.[17]

Already in the early 1960s, the Melikians had their eyes on Arizona. In 1964, the family traveled to Arizona by bus, wanting to have the boys see the U.S. countryside (the toddler Ramona was left in the care of Armenouhi, the Melikian grandmother). They rented a Volkswagen van in Arizona, and traveled throughout the state, spending a month at a rented residence off College Avenue adjacent to the campus of Arizona State University. The young boys enjoyed their stay in Arizona, including the swimming pool at their rented Tempe home.

It was also in the 1960s that Gregory began identifying potential property investment in Arizona, working with a Brooklyn World War II veteran and fellow lawyer transplant to Arizona, Raymond Hitzel.[18] Hitzel, who earlier had spent time with the Melikians during their 1964 travel to Ari-

dzFGeRpsTQ!2e0!6shttps:%2F%2Fstreetviewpixels-pa.googleapis.com%2Fv1%2Fthumb-nail%3Fpanoid%3DAABDoSmsxyCDdzFGeRpsTQ%26cb_client%3Dsearch.gws-prod.gps%26w%3D211%26h%3D120%26yaw%3D103.42726%26pitch%3D0%26thumbfov%3D100!7i16384!8i8192!4m14!1m7!3m6!1s0x89c261eb05847ebd:0x61c7bcf8e6b9266c!2sArmenian+Church+of+the+Holy+Martyrs!8m2!3d40.7462896!4d-73.7676985!16s%2F-g%2F1th5dh5r!3m5!1s0x89c261eb05847ebd:0x61c7bcf8e6b9266c!8m2!3d40.7462896!4d-73.7676985!16s%2Fg%2F1th5dh5r?entry=ttu (accessed 4 March 2024).
17. Emma Melikian interviewed by author on 20 September 2023.
18. "Raymond Hitzel Obituary," *Arizona Republic,* April 1, 2003.

zona, was one of a generation of real estate investors who helped feed the growth of the postwar Phoenix economy, built as it was in part on real estate development. Gregory began investing in Arizona, including property on Scottsdale Road toward Carefree and some in the Yuma area. Property values were always subject to volatility, and some who invested alongside the Melikians did not always secure immediate returns, but Gregory was patient, and the Arizona investments drew the Melikian family ever closer to the desert Southwest.

Emma and Gregory both recall a final symbolic turning point that triggered the family's ultimate move to Arizona.[19] In 1968, on one of their evenings at the Metropolian Opera in Lincoln Center, the couple was utterly unable to find a parking place. They ended up in some distant location so far from Lincoln Center that they were unable to locate their car at the end of the performance, finally returning home by taxi. Reflecting on the trauma of the evening, they asked each other whether it might not be less stressful, more pleasant to be living in the Phoenix valley, without the mad rush and traffic of New York City. There was some thought given to a winter residence in Phoenix, but Emma was concerned about the children's schooling which could not be interrupted during the academic year. In the months that followed their decision that evening to resettle in Phoenix, Gregory and Emma began to dispose of their property holdings in New York, ultimately including their residence on Beverly Road. Gregory traveled frequently between New York and Phoenix, and by the spring of 1969 the family was ready for its westward migration.

---

19. See the account also in the biography of Gregory Melikian by Lee B. Croft, *Peace and Preservation,* op. cit., p. 209-210.

4

America II – Phoenix

On 23 July 1969, the day of eldest son James's fourteenth birthday, Emma Ordjanian Melikian flew with her daughter Ramona to Phoenix, completing what was in effect a secondary, internal U.S. migration that followed by twenty-one years the earlier 1948 Ordjanian migration from Tehran to New York City. While Emma's world would change significantly in meeting the challenges of the desert southwest, there were remarkable continuities between her life in New York and that in Phoenix. Her world continued to revolve around her growing family, and she would again be thrust into ongoing issues of property management, remodeling, and interior design. Those were in part the legacies inherited from Tehran and New York—she was, after all, a daughter of property investor Samson Ordjanian, as well as a student trained in interior design, and the discerning wife and business partner of Gregory Melikian. She would continue her role as the multi-talented contributor to the Armenian diaspora and to philanthropy more generally. Emma even managed in Phoenix to expand on her Tehran and New York engagement with opera, although the opera world in Phoenix could never quite match her experience at "the Met." As a result of those continuities, Emma's years in Phoenix have never been about the displacement of her Tehran and New York worlds, but rather the reinterpretation and renewal of those worlds for the equally challenging environment of the desert southwest.

When Emma and Ramona arrived in Phoenix, Gregory and the three sons had preceded them, taking residence in a temporary apartment near

Camelback Road. By the end of 1969, the family had moved two additional times, once to a small three-bedroom house they purchased on White Gate Road, and finally to a permanent residence in the Arcadia district, this last a large modernist dwelling adjoining land immediately north of Camelback Road on the south side of Camelback Mountain (5020 North Arcadia Drive). The purchase of these houses was made possible by the sale of the Melikian home in Kew Gardens, with mortgage payments being met also from proceeds of the sale of their New York property holdings.

Gregory continued to travel frequently to New York to settle remaining property issues, and his law practice continued to function there for the better part of two years before he finally severed all remaining business ties in New York City. The result was that most local Phoenix family matters, including the renovation of their home on Camelback Mountain, fell to Emma. She recalls how Gregory, conscious of his absence from initial meetings with new family acquaintances, would later introduce himself in Phoenix with the expression, "Hello, I'm Gregory Melikian, the husband of Emma." Meanwhile, the Melikian children quickly settled into their new Arcadia home, having been enrolled in public schools in the fall of 1969—Arcadia High School for James; Hopi Elementary School for the three younger siblings.

Armenian Americans in Phoenix

Despite routine periods of separation while Gregory was in New York, the transition to Phoenix proceeded remarkably smoothly. The adjustment was made all the easier by the presence in Phoenix of acquaintances established prior to Gregory and Emma's departure from New York City. In the case of Gregory this included the real estate developer Raymond Hitzel. But, the Melikians also had established prior connections with the growing Armenian-American community in metropolitan Phoenix. Notable in that regard was the association with Mary and Steve Mehagian, owners of the Mehagian oriental rug, furniture, and design stores (Mehagian's Fine Furniture was a longstanding fixture on Central Avenue in Phoenix).

Born in the Ottoman Empire (Konya, Anatolia), Mary Mehagian (1903-2002) was the daughter of one of the most significant Armenian educators of the early twentieth century, the western-educated Dr. Armenag

Haigazian (1870-1921).[1] Emma first met Mary Haigazian Mehagian when Mary and her husband were in New York soliciting funds for what was then the new Haigazian College (founded 1955, in Beirut). Gregory and Emma contributed to the fund for the college and entertained the Mehagians at their home in Kew Gardens. Although the Mehagians, as well as the Mardian family in Phoenix,[2] hailed from Armenian Protestant backgrounds, not the Eastern rite Armenian Apostolic Church, their presence in Phoenix provided points of entry for the young Melikian family into the greater metropolitan Phoenix Armenian-American community. The Mehagians were also long-time supporters of the Armenian General Benevolent Union (AGBU) in the United States, founding a local chapter of AGBU in Phoenix.

Mary Mehagian (1903-2002) [3]

Toward the Building of St. Apkar Armenian Apostolic Church in Scottsdale

It was at one such gathering of AGBU, organized as an outdoor picnic in the early fall of 1969, that Emma was introduced to the larger community of Armenian Americans. Shortly after the AGBU gathering, Archbishop Torkom

---

1. The name of Armenag Haigazian and his work as an educator is very much associated with the growth of Armenian Protestantism in southwestern Anatolia in the early twentieth century and the work of the Union of the Armenian Evangelical Churches in the Near East (UAECNE) and the Armenian Missionary Association of America (AMAA). In the years before the Armenian genocide, Haigazian, who earned his Ph.D. in theology at Yale University, headed the Apostolic Institute in Konya (Jenanyan College, founded 1892). On Armenag Haigazian and Haigazian College (now, Haigazian University) in Beirut, see the account of "Our History and Heritage," within the Haigazian University website, http://www.haigazian.edu.lb/about-haigazian/our-history-heritage/, last accessed on 9 October 2023. On the early nineteenth-century establishment of Armenian Protestant communities in Ottoman lands, see Leon Arpee, "A Century of Armenian Protestantism," *Church History*, vol 5, no. 2 (June 1936), pp. 150-167.
2. The Mardian brothers owned one of the largest construction firms in Phoenix. Although Sam Mardian's tenure as mayor of Phoenix (1960-64) was prior to the Melikians arrival in the city, Gregory and Emma met the Mardians in 1969 and knew the brother Robert, a Republican activist and 1968 presidential campaign manager for Barry Goldwater. Robert Mardian was later indicted for his role in the Nixon Watergate scandal.
3. Photo is from Mary Mehagian obituary, *Arizona Republic*, 23 April 2002.

***St. Apkar Armenian Apostolic Church (Scottsdale, AZ), with Armenian Cultural
Center located to the right.***

(Manoogian), whom the Melikians had come to know during the building of the Holy Martyrs Armenian Church on Long Island, arrived at the Melikian home on Camelback Mountain for one of his informal visits in late fall 1969. Serving then as archbishop of the western diocese of the Armenian Church in America, Bishop Torkom used his visit to introduce Emma to Jerry Avakian, an electrical engineer born in Jerusalem who was also then new to the Phoenix valley. Emma would work closely with Jerry Avakian and his wife Joanne in gathering funds for a new Armenian church in the Phoenix valley. Bishop Torkom had earlier been in Phoenix to preside over an initial worship service held in 1963 when, with the help of Margaret Injasoulian (later, Emma's indefatigable friend "Marge"), the church was formally incorporated with the Arizona Corporation Commission. In the return visit of 1969, Bishop Torkom conducted a worship service for a large gathering at the Melikian home, the first such large indoor Armenian service. Attending the service at the Melikians' were the Hosepian sisters, Margaret and Atlanta, who later in the 1970s would donate the six acres of land on Cholla Road in Scottsdale that would become the site for the Armenian Cultural Center and St. Apkar's Armenian Apostolic Church.[4]

---

4. St. Apkar Armenian Apostolic Church in Scottsdale, Arizona (https://stapkar.com/) is named after Apkar V, one of the first Christian kings in history. Apkar had been converted to the faith by Thaddeus of Edessa, one of the seventy-two disciples or emissaries of Christ referenced in the Gospel of Luke (10:1). According to the historian Eusebius, Apkar exchanged correspondence with Jesus in the early first century. Although King Apkar is claimed by Armenians as one of their own, he was an Arab or Armenian dynast ruling over the Arab community in Edessa in the upper Mesopotamian region. See J. B. Segal, "Abgar," *Encyclopædia Iranica*, I/2, pp. 210-213, and online at https://iranicaonline.org/articles/abgar-dynasty-of-edessa-2nd-century-bc-to-3rd-century-ad, last accessed on 12

Thus, within months of the Melikians' migration to Phoenix, Emma was drawn into efforts that would later culminate in the building, first, of the church's large Armenian Cultural Center (1992), and then of St. Apkar church (consecrated 2009). Emma and her son Robert served on the building committee for the Cultural Center. Eldest son James served on the church council. Gregory and Emma joined Emma's brother Nikit in making substantial donations to the fund for the building's construction. The Mardian construction company erected the building (one of the Mardian brothers, John, also served on the building committee). Emma added her own design features to the Cultural Center, notably in the attractive octagonal entry and the second-floor library named for Nikit and Eleanora Ordjanian. On the recommendation of the building committee's chair, Marge Injasoulian, the main Cultural Center hall was named for the Melikians—Melikian Hall. Emma was less focused on the naming of the building, and recalls rather her own and Jerry Avakian's visits to local Armenian-American homes desperately seeking contributions to meet monthly mortgage payments for the Cultural Center.

"Marge" Injasoulian
(1936-2015) [5]

Introduction to Arizona State University

Beyond the immediate Armenian-American community, Emma's new Arizona world entailed challenges in the fall of 1969 that were quite unexpected. "Out of the blue," as she recounts, Emma was contacted by Rachel Lauterpacht, widow of the British international jurist and human rights champion, Sir Hersch Lauterpacht (1897-1960).[6] The Melikians had met

October 2023. Apkar was also the name of the father of the Hosepian sisters who donated the Scottsdale land for the Armenian church in Arizona.

5. Photo is from the Injasoulian obituary, *Arizona Republic,* 11 November 2015.

6. Sir Hersch Lauterpacht, born in a small shtetl in Galicia in 1897, became one of the most distinguished international lawyers of the twentieth century, serving at the end of World War II as a member of the British War Crimes Executive and on the British legal team at the Nuremberg Trials in 1946. The Whewell Chair of International Law at Cambridge University, he was the author of *An International Bill of the Rights of Man* (1945) and *International Law and Human Rights* (1950), and served for many years as the editor of the *British Yearbook of International Law*. He was knighted in 1956. It was much earlier

the Lauterpachts at a United Nations event many years earlier in New York, but Emma had maintained only sporadic communication with Lady Lauterpacht after the 1960 death of her husband. Suddenly, Emma received word by note and in a follow-on telephone call that Rachel Lauterpacht was planning a visit to Phoenix in connection with her decision to donate the personal library holdings of her late husband to the Arizona State University College of Law. Lady Lauterpacht asked if Emma could accompany her around Phoenix and assist in making local arrangements for the visit.

By the time Rachel Lauterpacht arrived in Phoenix, arrangements were completed for the transfer of the Lauterpacht personal library holdings to the ASU College of Law Library, one of the foundational bequests for the relatively new law college's library holdings. It was during the visit of Lady Lauterpacht to Phoenix that Emma first visited the campus of Arizona State University, joining her distinguished visitor in meetings at the ASU College of Law. What these initial ties and visits demonstrated, including the Lauterpacht visit and the ties to the Armenian-American diaspora in Phoenix, was the generous, welcoming spirit that has always attracted people to Emma. The warmth of her welcome, her generous recognition of others, and her genuine affection for those whom she met led to a growing circle of friends already in the first year of her residence in Phoenix. On the occasion of the 1970 New Year's Day reception she hosted for Steve Mehagian's 75th birthday—a celebration

Lady Rachel Lauterpacht (1901-1989) Edited photo is courtesy of the Melikian Family Archive.

---

as a doctoral student in Vienna that he met his future wife, Rachel Steinberg (sister-in-law of Israeli Foreign Minister Abba Eban), who had traveled to Vienna from her home in the Palestine Mandate to study piano. On Sir Hersch Lauterpacht, see the biography written by his son Elihu Lauterpacht, also an international legal scholar, entitled *The Life of Hersch Lauterpacht* (Cambridge U Press, 2010). The bulk of the vast Lauterpacht international law library holdings (100 meters in length) was donated to Gray's Inn where the son, Sir Elihu Lauterpacht, was a distinguished fellow (see "The Lauterpacht Collection," https:// www.lcil.cam.ac.uk/sites/www.law.cam.ac.uk/files/images/www.lcil.law.cam.ac.uk/Documents/the_lauterpacht_collection_-_march_2020_update_pdf.pdf, last accessed on 26 October 2023). But the private, personal library holdings of Sir Hersch Lauterpacht were donated to the ASU College of Law Library.

that included the Bimsons, Herbergers, and a wide gathering of others from Phoenix society—Mary Mehagian commented to Emma, "How in the world did you manage to meet all these people?!" Indeed—for Emma had moved to Phoenix less than six months prior.

Opera in Phoenix

Somewhat more daunting was the challenge posed by the opera scene in Phoenix. Within a year of their arrival in Phoenix, Emma and Gregory decided to attend the performance of a visiting opera troupe from San Diego, there being no local opera company performing in metropolitan Phoenix. The performance was held in a west side high school gymnasium, and the quality of the performance was very poor—"horrible," according to Emma. Upon further inquiry, they discovered that there was a new professional opera company in Tucson—the Tucson Opera—which had been launched in 1971 with the support of the University of Arizona arts community under the direction of James (Jim) Sullivan (1936-2020), a Ph.D. music student at the University of Arizona. Sullivan served as director of the Tucson Opera for its first ten years during which time the Tucson Opera expanded to become the Arizona Opera with a full season of performances each year in both Tucson and Phoenix. Working with a group of Tucson opera supporters, including Patty DeConcini (wife of U.S. Senator Dennis DeConcini), the Melikians, the Bimsons, and the Jochums, among others, supported the transformation of Tucson Opera into the Arizona Opera, which completed its first full season in Phoenix in 1976-77.

The Arizona Opera became one of a handful of opera companies nationally to perform regularly in more than one city. Having produced more than two hundred operas and concerts since its 1971 inaugural year, the Arizona Opera presented Wagner's complete Ring Cycle twice, a feat only accomplished in North America by four other companies.[7] It was during the tail end of the Sullivan directorship that Gregory Melikian began his service as chair of the Arizona Opera Board of Directors, serving in that capacity from the late 1970s through the early 1980s. During those years, the Melikians came to relish the visit of great singers who came to offer benefit concerts, including performances in Phoenix of the renowned opera tenors, Luciano

---

7. See https://azopera.org/about/arizona-opera-history, last accessed on 26 October 2023.

Pavarotti and Placido Domingo. Emma recalls with some pride the fact that, during Gregory's tenure as board chair, the Arizona Opera was able to lure Glynn Ross from the Seattle Opera in 1983 to serve as director of the Arizona Opera. Born Glynn Aus of Scandinavian immigrant parents, the enterprising Ross served as director until his retirement in 1998, both expanding the company's offerings and restoring it to financial health. It may not have been The Met, but Arizona Opera was a serious professional performing company—a source of great satisfaction for Gregory and Emma. It was

through the Arizona Opera that Gregory and Emma also came to know and cherish the friendship of opera buff Rabbi Albert Plotkin. The beloved Rabbi Plotkin once joined the Melikians on an extended cruise when they were touring around the world, but Emma always remembers Plotkin for his voice. "Who can forget," Emma recalls, "the time when Rabbi Plotkin came on the Arizona Opera stage as the king in the closing moments of Puccini's 'Turandot' to sing the short baritone aria, 'May Love Prevail.'"[8]

Glynn Ross, 1914-2005 [9]

Fittingly, when Arizona Opera began performing in Phoenix in the late 1970s and 1980s, the San Carlos Hotel, acquired by the Melikians in 1973, became the residence for the Arizona Opera with the Melikians providing free lodging while the company performed annually in Phoenix. The lobby of the hotel became rehearsal space.

Rabbi Albert Plotkin, 1920-2010 [10]

---

8. Emma remembers fondly how Rabbi Plotkin used to join the Melikian family on Christmas Eve in the years following his wife Sylvia's death in 1996. During one of the Melikians' round-the-world cruises, Rabbi Plotkin and the Melikians' son Richard joined the cruise in Australia, replacing Emma who returned to Phoenix. Rabbi Plotkin affectionately spoke of Richard Melikian as "My Rick."
9. Photo is courtesy of Bruce Duffie, "Administrator Glynn Ross, 1914-2005," at http://www.bruceduffie.com/ross.html, accessed 6 March 2024.
10. Photo is from the 2010 obituary for Rabbi Plotkin *Jewish News of Northern California,* at https://jweekly.com/2010/02/12/dea1/, accessed 6 March 2024.

Arizona Property Acquisitions

Serving a far wider audience than the Arizona Opera, the San Carlos Hotel in downtown Phoenix became a small part of a Melikian commercial real estate enterprise that extended throughout Arizona, including properties in Tucson, Flagstaff, Scottsdale, Holbrook, and Phoenix. For twenty years, beginning in the 1970s, Emma was a licensed real estate broker, serving as a working partner in the Melikian real estate enterprise that operated in Arizona under a variety of general titles, including Great Western Realty, Great Western Associates (from 1983) and Melikian Enterprises (from 1996). In one sense, this was an activity well known to Emma, managing property investments much as the Ordjanian and Melikian enterprises in New York. But in New York the investments had been largely in apartment buildings and family dwellings. In Arizona, while there continued to be investment and remodeling of the family dwelling on Arcadia Drive in Phoenix, Melikian Arizona investments focused largely on commercial property, especially buildings with a distinctive historical or period character.

Hotel San Carlos, Phoenix, Arizona. Courtesy of Melikian Family Archive

The interest in historic properties was notable in the case of the 1973 purchase of Hotel San Carlos, a downtown Phoenix landmark built in 1927-28 in the Renaissance-Revival style.[11] The interest in period architec-

11. For a splendid historical and pictorial overview of the San Carlos, see the work of Robert A. Melikian, *Hotel San Carlos* (Arcadia Publishing: Charleston/Chicago/San Francisco,

ture was also reflected in the historic properties purchased in Tucson. The three-story Old Pueblo Club Building (111 S. Stone Ave., built in 1908) and the original Art Deco Sears Building (6th Avenue, built in 1924), both in downtown Tucson, are examples of historic buildings purchased by the Melikians and remodeled for modern office space. In Scottsdale, the Melikians purchased an old Mormon Church (3080 N. Civic Center Plaza), converting it into offices. Emma found herself drawn into the major remodeling projects necessitated by the purchase of these historic buildings. All the while, these property investments were appreciating in value, generating rental income, and ultimately yielding profitable sales that permitted Gregory and Emma to continue their philanthropy while providing support for the family.

Old Pueblo Club, Tucson, Arizona [12]

2009), especially pp. 43ff.

12. Photo is from Google Maps (2024) at https://www.google.com/maps/place/The+Historic+Old+Pueblo+Club+Building/@32.2204574,-110.9709581,3a,90y,104.11h,117.76t/data=!3m6!1e1!3m4!1sqhUDAZKmFbyfOKqqdIOWCg!2e0!7i16384!8i8192!4m14!1m7!3m6!1s0x86d671f903fde037:0xebe6af65c6cc7995!2sThe+Historic+Old+Pueblo+Club-+Building!8m2!3d32.2203052!4d-110.9708649!16s%2Fg%2F11gzs7h-ngl!3m5!1s0x86d671f903fde037:0xebe6af65c6cc7995!8m2!3d32.2203052!4d-110.9708649!16s%2Fg%2F11gzs7hngl?entry=ttu, accessed 6 March 2024.

Original Downtown Sears Building, Tucson [13]

Abandoned Mormon Church, Scottsdale, AZ [14]

---

13. Photo is from Rick Wiley, "'Sears Stores in Tucson Since 1928" (13 February 2023), at https://tucson.com/news/local/photos-sears-stores-in-tucson-since-1928/collection_e2ee39a6-a997-11ed-acb5-ff20ef9beb56.html#1, accessed 6 March 2024.

14. Photo is from "List of Historic Properties in Scottsdale, Arizona," *Wikipedia* (https://en.wikipedia.org/wiki/List_of_historic_properties_in_Scottsdale,_Arizona, accessed 6 March 2024).

Mormon Church remodeled (today) [15]

Occasionally, as in the case of the Hotel San Carlos in downtown Phoenix for which they carried the mortgage when selling it in 1979, the Melikians would recover properties once sold when buyers were no longer able to sustain payments. Hotel San Carlos was first sold on the eve of the Melikians' twenty-fifth wedding anniversary in 1979, shortly before Gregory and Emma embarked on the first of their significant international travels. What they discovered upon return to Phoenix was that they would regain the hotel, becoming second-time owners of the property. Whether by recovering forfeited property or capitalizing on significant property appreciation in value, the Melikian real estate enterprise was professionally managed and profitable at a time when the major Arizona urban centers of Phoenix and Tucson were undergoing rapid growth and commercial property vacancy rates were unusually low. With Emma's remodeling efforts and the Melikian sons' increasingly active managerial leadership—Richard, for example, took major responsibilities for managing Tucson properties, and the three sons from the 1980s took joint responsibility for all purchase decisions—the Melikian real estate enterprise became an extraordinarily successful family business.

World Travel

From their initial telephone conversations in New York City prior to their engagement, Gregory and Emma shared a deep interest in interna-

---

15. Photo is edited from Google Maps (2024) at https://www.google.com/maps/place/3080+N+Civic+Center+Plaza,+Scottsdale,+AZ+85251/@33.483564,-111.9223387,17z/data=!3m1!4b1!4m6!3m5!1s0x872b0bc4a772cfb7:0xea4a4b620513eb91!8m2!3d33.483564!4d-111.9223387!16s%2Fg%2F11bw3_5k43?entry=ttu, accessed 6 March 2024.

tional affairs, and specifically in international travel and adventure. But they had had little time for such travel in the early years of their marriage when work and family considerations kept them from extensive overseas travel. Emma was not just nurturing a family of four growing children, she was also attending to the care of the couple's two widowed mothers who, along with Emma's sister Isabella and brother-in-law Levon Karapetian, had followed the family to Phoenix. That all changed in 1979 when Emma and Gregory, marking their twenty-fifth wedding anniversary, departed on a vacation trip to western Europe—their first return to Europe in more than thirty years. Gregory had not spent time in Europe since his remarkable World War II service as a telegraph operator in Allied Command Headquarters in France,[16] and Emma was last in Paris during the Ordjanian family migration to New York City in 1948.

During the course of the following twenty years at regular intervals throughout the remainder of the twentieth century, Emma and Gregory logged in major international travels to western Europe (including Ireland and Scandinavia), the Soviet Union, the Balkans, Egypt, Israel, the Sinai desert, the Mediterranean, South America, West Africa, Southeast Asia, and China, in addition to two round-the-world travels that took them to Australia, South Asia, and the Suez Canal. On top of this, there were cruises to Canada and through the St. Lawrence Seaway. Travels were the occasion for meeting with old friends and making new ones, while renewing ties with distant family.

In the case of the separate travel to the Soviet Union that followed their trip to western Europe in 1979, the journey took Emma and Gregory not only to Moscow, Leningrad, and Central Asia, but also to parts of the USSR where they managed to meet with those members of the Rustamian family (Emma's maternal side) who had remained in Rostov-on-Don and in Yerevan, Armenia. In Rostov-on-Don, the Melikians stayed at an international hotel on Pushkin Street directly across the street from the former delicatessen operated by her maternal grandparents in the Russian Empire. While Emma was overjoyed to connect for the first time with family on her mother's side, the 1979 travel in the Soviet Union also reinforced many of the concerns raised by her father about Communist disregard for basic civil liberties, and the consequent fear local residents shared in hosting western

16. On Gregory Melikian's legendary service in World War II, see Lee B. Croft, *Peace and Preservation,* pp. 37-139.

visitors, even in the case of close family. Emma's brother Nikit had continued to send money to family members in the Soviet Union, and the Melikians were understandably well received. Emma's ability to communicate in Russian with family no doubt contributed greatly to the success of such visits. But Emma recalls how uneasy she felt about monetary exchanges with family that threatened to turn joyous reunions into embarrassing reminders of the cross-cultural inequalities separating diaspora from homeland.

Among the highpoints in these international travels, Emma recalls two visits in particular that were riveting. She regrets only that, despite her interest in photography, she did not manage to capture the full force of such visits. The first of those visits was to Egypt, Israel, and the Sinai desert—a visit that followed the Camp David Accords and the full recognition and exchange of ambassadors between Israel and Egypt in January/February 1980. Even following mutual diplomatic recognition, flights between Israel and Egypt remained complicated, especially for those wishing to visit the ancient site of St. Catherine's Monastery in the Sinai Peninsula.

St. Catherine's, the oldest continually inhabited monastic site in Christendom, rests at the foot of Mount Sinai where it is claimed that Moses received the Tablets of the Law and saw the burning bush. Built by the Byzantine Emperor Justinian I, the monastery dates from the middle of the sixth century A.D.[17] For their visit Gregory and Emma had to fly into Sharm El Sheik from Tel Aviv, and then go by car to the site of the monastery. The monastic site is important not just for its ancient icons and historic location, but because it houses the oldest continually active library repository in the world, dating as it does from the sixth century. Among its unusually rare holdings, the Library of St. Catherine's Monastery held, until the nineteenth century, the Codex Sinaiticus, the oldest complete manuscript edition of the Bible dating from the fourth century A.D. Shrouded in intrigue—the disappearance of the Codex Sinaiticus in the nineteenth century, its reappearance in Russia, and subsequent sale to the British Library by Stalin in 1933—the manuscript is one small part of the remarkable history of St. Catherine's. Emma recalls being carried up on a basket to the holy mountains surrounding the famous monastic site.

----

17. Since 2002, St. Catherine's Monastery is a UNESCO World Heritage Site. For a general description, see "St. Catherine Area," prepared by the UNESCO World Heritage Convention, https://whc.unesco.org/en/list/954, last accessed 30 October 2023.

St. Catherine's Monastery, Mt. Sinai [18]

A second encounter, no less striking, dates from the Melikians' round-the-world travel in 1983 with their friends Grant and Shireen Malouf and Larry Ward, founder of the charitable organization, Food for the Hungry.[19] One of the sites visited on the travel was Calcutta, India, where Larry Ward took Emma and Gregory to the site of Mother Theresa's Kalighat Home for the Dying Destitute.[20] Mother Theresa happened to be at the Kalighat Home when the visitors arrived. The Melikians were led in to meet with her amidst all those destitute and dying for whom Mother Theresa and her sisters of mercy were caring. Emma was surprised that Mother Theresa was notably interested in talking about the Melikians' Armenian roots, a matter in which Mother Theresa took great interest. In retrospect, there has been

---

18. Photo of St. Catherine's Monastery is from "St. Catherine's Monastery" on the Britannica's website, https://www.britannica.com/topic/Saint-Catherines-Monastery, accessed 6 March 2024.

19. Food for the Hungry is a Christian humanitarian aid and global development organization that seeks to address the problem of world hunger and the underlying root causes of poverty. Its founder Larry Ward began the organization in California in 1971, but in 1974 moved its administrative offices to Phoenix where he met the Melikians. On Food for the Hungry, see their website, https://www.fh.org/, last accessed 30 October 2023.

20. There is a huge literature on Mother Theresa, who was consecrated St. Theresa in 2016. She was awarded the Nobel Peace Prize in 1979. The female Catholic nuns of Missionaries of Charity, an order she founded, took as their mission the care for the dying on the streets of Calcutta, where the Kalighat Home for the Dying Destitute is located. Among many biographies of her, see Anne Sebba, *Mother Teresa: Beyond the Image* (New York: Doubleday, 1997).

speculation that Mother Theresa's father, Nikollë Bojaxhiu (1874-1919), a businessman and pharmacist in Skopje (North Macedonia), may have been Armenian by origin, leading Emma to wonder whether the interest that Mother Theresa showed in her may have related to distant family origins.[21] In any event, Emma's visit with the saintly Mother Theresa at the Home for the Dying Destitute left an indelible impression. During that same travel, Emma and Gregory visited Rangoon where they were met and greeted in Armenian by Father Felix, the Indian parish priest of the Armenian church in Burma (now Myanmar).

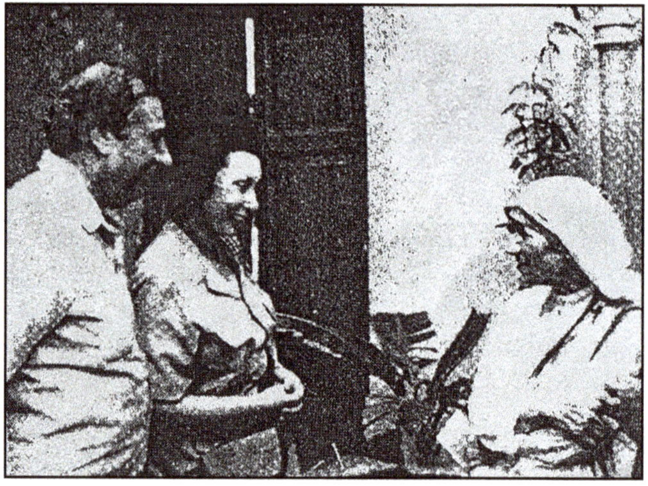

Gregory and Emma Melikian with Mother Theresa in Calcutta
Photo courtesy of the Melikian Family Archive

For Emma Ordjanian Melikian, international travel not only brought new acquaintances, but it also satisfied an elemental curiosity. She was now an American patriot, a successful immigrant in an adopted American new

---

21. The rumor that Emma refers to is one that claims Mother Theresa's father was really an Armenian with distant family from western Armenia under the surname Boyajian, not Bojaxhiu. That claim began to spread after the visit of Mother Theresa to Armenia following the Spitak earthquake of 1988. During that visit, Mother Theresa is thought to have remarked to the Etchmiadzin Armenian Catholicos Vazgen I that her father was of Armenian parentage (see http://www.noravank.am/eng/news/detail.php?ELEMENT_ID=14974, last accessed 30 October 2023). While many pharmacists in the Balkans did tend to be of Armenian origin, Mother Theresa's father, who was multi-lingual, did not speak Armenian. He may have had distant family from western Armenia, but he is generally considered to have been an Albanian or Vlach/Aromanian Catholic born in the Kosovar town of Prizren.

world. And yet, she was still that inquisitive sojourner, operating creatively between a world fashioned in Iran and a new world that included extended and immediate family, property responsibilities, longstanding religious and ethnic allegiances, and international engagement. Her curiosity was grounded in a generous, welcoming appreciation for "the other." In Phoenix, the welcomed "other" could be a distinguished international visitor, a representative from a Phoenix sister city, a fellow Armenian immigrant, or a prominent university president. But it also was reflected in an empathy for those less fortunate, a generosity no doubt reinforced in the 1983 meeting with Mother Theresa. In the 1990s, it was the concern and identification with those less fortunate that would take on renewed importance as Emma founded her own charitable NGO (non-governmental organization) to address the immigrant experience and her need to "give back" to her adopted American homeland. That is the story of Thank You America.

Thank You America

As Emma tells the story, Thank You America began on an unseasonably cold winter day in early 1992 on the corner of Camelback Road and 44th Street in Phoenix. On her way downtown, Emma was traveling in her warm car when she caught site of a woman in a sun dress, quite unprepared for the winter cold, clutching a young infant on the busy corner. Emma turned the corner, parked her car, and got out to approach the woman with the idea of providing her own warm coat for the shivering stranger. But, by the time she had managed to get back to the woman at the corner, the stranger was no longer there, probably having been picked up by a passing bus.

Nevertheless, the sight of the struggling woman in the cold stuck with Emma, who was mortified by such poverty and homelessness in a country of obvious abundance, and she determined to do something about it, reflecting as she did on the comment she had just heard on the radio that "charity begins at home." Upon returning home, she recalls asking her son Robert to help her right away, first, in gathering blankets for the homeless shelter CASS, and second, in establishing with the Arizona Corporation Commission a 501(c)3 non-profit charitable organization that could feature immigrant Americans giving back to their adopted American homeland. By July 1992, Thank You America, as it came to be called, was formally established as a non-profit corporation, or foundation. Emma Melikian was its president, her friend Jerry Avakian was the vice-president, and Ramona Melikian was its secretary. Emma's sister Isabella Karapetian was listed along with Jerry Avakian and Emma on the board of directors.

From its founding in 1992, Thank You America had two distinguishing features. First, it sought to identify and lift up the immigrant experience, including the rich cultural heritage of first- and second-generation Arizona immigrants. In an Arizona political context this was a remarkably audacious goal, seeking as it did to extol the virtues of immigrants in a state in which politicians too often sought to stigmatize for political gain the immigrant.[22] Second, Thank You America sought to mobilize the Arizona immigrant community to "give back" to those less fortunate in their adopted American homeland.

There were multiple efforts to fulfill the first goal of identifying and lifting up the immigrant communities of Arizona. The most high profile of these efforts was the annual Festival of Nations sponsored by Thank You America on the square formerly located outside Phoenix Symphony Hall. The Festival of Nations was typically held on the weekend immediately prior to the week of Thanksgiving Day. For the event, Thank You America would invite ethnic communities of Arizona to establish booths and contribute to a set of program events (including ethnic dances, music, fashion, etc.). The festival was publicized throughout metropolitan Phoenix. In 1998, Scottsdale Mayor Sam Campana, seeing the success of the Phoenix festival, invited Thank You America to join a parallel weekend festival that Scottsdale had been holding in Scottsdale Civic Plaza Center for several years. These annual Festival of Nations events drew sizable crowds of immigrants, as well as the public at large.

---

22. The culmination of this anti-immigrant fever came in 2010 with the Arizona State Legislature's enactment of Senate Bill 1070, signed into law by Governor Jan Brewer, which made it a misdemeanor for an alien to be in Arizona without carrying registration certification, and requiring state law enforcement officers to attempt to determine an individual's immigration status during any "lawful stop, detention or arrest" when there is reasonable suspicion that the individual is an illegal immigrant. The law, which had the effect of stigmatizing Arizona's immigrant population, generated immigrant fear of being apprehended and deported for failure to be able to prove their lawful immigrant status. Federal Judge Susan Bolton issued a preliminary injunction shortly before the act was to go into effect, blocking the law's most egregious provisions, but in 2012 the U.S. Supreme Court (*Arizona v. United States*) upheld the provision requiring immigration status checks during law enforcement stops. On SB 1070, see the special virtual issue of *Social Science Quarterly* devoted to "Immigration on the One Year Anniversary of Arizona SB 1070," 2011 (*Social Science Quarterly* is the organ of the Southwest Social Science Association).

In addition to launching the annual festival, Thank You America sponsored an annual children's art contest, working with a local Scottsdale school to reward the finest 7th and 8th grade posters inspired by the question, "What the American flag Means to Me." In a periodic newsletter under the editorship of Emma's daughter Ramona (titled *One Unified Voice*), feature essays were solicited from prominent immigrants and updates on previous and forthcoming Thank You America events were highlighted.

These expressions of patriotism could be very inspiring. However, the effort was not without detractors. Emma recalls her effort to solicit a newsletter essay from the celebrated Italian-American architect

Masthead of Thank You America Newsletter, courtesy of Melikian Family Archive.

and creator of Arizona's *Arcosanti* site, Paolo Soleri. Unaware at the time of the charges of his misogyny and sexual abuse that would later surface,[23] Emma, who admired Soleri's bells and was interested in his concept of *arcology* (the integration of architecture and ecology), approached the immigrant Soleri in person, asking him if he would contribute his own essay "on the meaning of the American flag" for publication in the Thank You America newsletter. His sharply cynical retort, which must have been unexpected and disappointing for Emma, was simply, "I don't believe in flags."

Perhaps nothing so clearly encapsulated the celebratory side of Thank You America as well as the speeches Emma was invited to give at ceremonies held for newly naturalized citizens in Phoenix. No doubt having been invited to give such a greeting because of her work with Thank You America, Emma addressed the 1997 naturalization ceremony in words that have

---

23. On this dark side of Soleri, see Steve Rose, "'His Inner Circle Knew of the Abuse': Daniela Soleri on Her Architect Father Paolo," *The Guardian,* 29 February 2020 (online at https://www.theguardian.com/artanddesign/2020/feb/29/paolo-soleri-architect-abuser-arcosanti-utopian-city-steve-rose, last accessed on 4 December 2023).

been transcribed and passed down within the family. Addressing her comments to the new citizens in front of her, Emma spoke autobiographically:

> Your Honor, members of the court, ladies and gentlemen, fellow Americans, Congratulations! Today is one of the most important chapters in your life, you are now an American citizen, free to pursue your happiness and dreams. Your rights are only limited by the rights of others. This is the only country in the world that opens its arms, takes us in, and gives us the rights that a native-born American has. What a country!
>
> I know how all of you citizens are feeling right now. I am an immigrant just like you. I am of Armenian heritage and my parents escaped communism and fled from Russia to Iran in 1932, where I was born. As a child, every time I saw the American flag or heard the national anthem, my body broke out in goose bumps and I thought of hope and freedom.
>
> In 1948, my whole family and I were fortunate enough to enter the USA and in 1955 [sic, 1954], I became an American citizen, just like you today. My becoming an American citizen did not mean that I forgot my heritage or traditions. I should hold onto that because it makes me a better human being, and a better citizen. I respect and honor my heritage, but now I am an American just like you. And this is my home, just like yours. And this is my country, as it is yours.
>
> Now we must learn the traditions, the heritage, and the language of this beloved country. If we do not it means that we do not respect this land that has accepted us. . . .
>
> It does not matter if you are English, if you are Irish, if you are Mexican, Chinese, Korean, Italian, Filipino, or anything else—You are an American! It does not matter if you are black, brown, white, yellow, or red. We are all Americans!
>
> . . . With our unified strength, we have the opportunity to show our gratitude to this country by bringing the important values of our ancestors--values like hard work, respect, responsibility, and the importance of family.
>
> Today you take your first step on a journey that will change the course of your life and that of this country. As President

Kennedy said, "Ask not what your country can do for you, but what you can do for your country." God bless you all! Congratulations! And Thank You America![24]

The closing theme in the speech—that of expressing one's gratitude— was the second pillar of the Thank You America project, and Emma was particularly engaged in this effort to give back. Her special focus was on young people, future generations. Toward that end, Thank You America began addressing the needs of homeless children, linking itself with the Thomas J. Pappas Regional Education Center for the Homeless in Phoenix. Named for the late Thomas J. Pappas (d. 1989), a prominent Phoenix businessman, the Pappas School system sought to identify and train homeless children in a practical school environment geared to the special needs of itinerant homeless kids, including the establishment of scholastic and health records for the homeless children it served.[25] A part of the Maricopa County Regional School District, the Pappas Regional Education Center became a magnet school, providing primary and secondary education to homeless children. The project had its origins in 1989 when Phoenix firefighters became involved in tutoring homeless kids as a charity project. This expanded into regular county-supported schooling under the superintendency of Sandra Dowling, long-time head of the Maricopa County Regional School District.

One of the most intractable problems that the Pappas school system faced was that of locating and ferrying itinerant homeless children to its facilities. Emma was convinced that it would be easier to address this prob-

---

24. "Speech Given by Emma Melikian, President and Founder of the Thank You America Foundation, at the 1997 Naturalization Ceremony, Phoenix, AZ." The full speech is preserved in the Melikian Family Archive.

25. For a brief overview of the Pappas School system, see "A Magnet for Homeless Students: The Thomas J. Pappas Regional Education Center," online at https://eric.ed.gov/?id=EJ498881, last accessed on 4 December 2023. The Pappas School system was closed in 2008 following highly publicized allegations over misuse of funds and corruption in the Maricopa County Regional School District. County officials claimed, not without challenge, that the homeless students in the system might better be mainstreamed in regular public schools. On the funding controversy, see Pat Flannery, "Financial probe of superintendent criticized as politics," *The Arizona Republic,* 27 January 2006. County officials had sought to tar the Maricopa County School Superintendent, Sandra Dowling, whose support for the Pappas School was well known. Dowling was eventually cleared of all charges. She sued Maricopa County for bringing false charges against her and was awarded a cash settlement in 2013.

lem if the Pappas School system had its own vans to bring children from under bridges, from homeless shelters, and from the streets to the Pappas education center. Collaborating with Joe Gambino, the Sicilian-born owner of Gateway Chevrolet, Emma secured discounts on the purchase of two Chevrolet vans for Thank You America that were then used to locate and ferry homeless kids to the Pappas school system throughout the 1990s.[26]

To enrich the training for students in the Pappas Schools, Emma enlisted and supported the introduction of Tumbleweed Youth Development training at Pappas School. The Tumbleweed Center for Youth Development, launched in Phoenix in 1972, continues to the present, offering programs "to meet the challenges of adolescence and adulthood through a coordinated, progressive series of activities and experiences which help them to become socially, morally, emotionally, physically and cognitively competent."[27] Emma arranged for Tumbleweed to offer basic skills and entrepreneurship training at the Pappas Schools.

The programs sponsored by Thank You America for Pappas Schools, including the work with Tumbleweed and other children's support initiatives, required financial resources that Emma optimistically thought could be generated by tapping into the same immigrant communities whose rich cultural diversity she sought to showcase. As Emma put it, "There were in the 1990s about 250,000 first-generation immigrants in Arizona. If each of them was to give one dollar, Thank You America could operate very successfully." But, in reality, almost all the funding for Thank You America came from the Melikians' own family resources. As Emma notes, "Gregory and the family were always very supportive." In particular, Emma's daughter Ramona was essential to the operation, editing and publishing the newsletter and assisting with all manner of personal contacts. Ramona's earlier experience working with the Council on Foreign Relations in New

---

26. See the obituary for Joe Gambino prepared by Russ Wiles, "Phoenix-area Chevrolet dealer Joe Gambino, a 'self-made man,' dies at 88," *Arizona Republic,* 27 July 2019, online at https://www.azcentral.com/story/money/business/entrepreneurs/2019/07/27/joe-gambino-owner-gateway-chevrolet-phoenix-area-dies-88/1768305001/, last accessed on 4 December 2023.

27. On the Tumbleweed Center for Youth Development, see their website, http://www.tumbleweed.org/youth_development.html, last accessed on 4 December 2023. Tumbleweed's Youth Crisis Shelter, a short-term crisis intervention program for homeless and runaway youth ages 9-18 opened in 1975. Since 2005, Tumbleweed has been the lead local agency under contract with a national program called "Safe Place" providing "access to immediate help and supportive resources for young people in crisis through a network of sites sustained by qualified agencies, trained volunteers, and businesses."

York City and as an intern for the Armenian Assembly in Washington, DC, prepared her well for what was often the daily work of facilitating Thank You America operations. Accordingly, when Ramona married and moved to California in 1999, Emma scaled back Thank You America operations. The last Festival of Nations held with Thank You America sponsorship was in November 1998, and Emma effectively phased out her involvement with her foundation thereafter.

In 1999, both the local Phoenix chapter of the Daughters of the American Revolution and the national Freedoms Foundation at Valley Forge conferred on Emma Ordjanian Melikian their distinguished service award for her charitable efforts on behalf of Thank You America. In the case of the Freedoms Foundation's "Distinguished Citizen Award," Emma was one of eight hundred names nominated for the prestigious national award. The closure of Thank You America did not mark the end of Emma's philanthropy. The charitable commitment highlighted in Thank You America, notably her concern for the "next generation" and her desire to maintain connection with her immigrant heritage, would soon resurface in the early years of the twenty-first century when she and Gregory began a significant new investment in partnership with Arizona State University.

5

Emma Melikian and the ASU Melikian Center

After arriving in metropolitan Phoenix in 1969, Gregory and Emma Melikian were regular contributors to Arizona State University (ASU). Not only had their three sons graduated with multiple degrees from ASU, but the Melikian family had also been supporters of the university's KAET public television station (the first organizational meeting of the Friends of Channel 8 was held at the Melikian home), and Gregory and Emma had made contributions to the ASU School of Music.

For Emma, there was a family history associated with major contributions to American higher education. Her brother Nikit, an engineer and founder of Columbia Technical Corporation in New York, was active in the Armenian-American community and a leader in the effort to establish the Armenian Center at Columbia University. For more than a decade, beginning in 1977, Nikit chaired the Advisory Council for Armenian Studies at Columbia, a position he was appointed to by Columbia University President William McGill. Nikit and his wife Eleanora were among the leading benefactors supporting the development of Armenian Studies at Columbia. From 1979 onward, distinguished scholars have been honored to hold the Nikit Ordjanian Chair in Armenian History and Civilization at Columbia.[1]

---

1. See the brochure, "The Armenian Presence at Columbia University: Tenth Anniversary,"

Beginning in 2001, both the focus and the level of Melikian family support for Arizona State University changed significantly. Drawn to the programming of ASU's Critical Languages Institute (CLI)—a nationally recognized summer program within the ASU Russian and East European Studies Center (REESC) for intensive study of less commonly taught languages—Emma and Gregory Melikian welcomed a proposal from REESC to establish, with Melikian support, Armenian language training within the Center's CLI. The initial Melikian Fund of $30,000 was intended to support a three-year pilot CLI instructional program in Eastern Armenian. That gift began a process of collaboration and financial investment (more than $1 million) that, in December 2006, culminated in the renaming of the ASU Russian and East European Studies Center—henceforth, the Melikian Center: Russian, Eurasian, and East European Studies at ASU.[2]

To understand the history of The Melikian Center and the significance and timing of Emma Melikian's role in it, it is worth reviewing the pre-history of the Melikian Center, which dated to the 1970s. Within U.S. higher education, international area study centers faced major crosscurrents in the last quarter of the twentieth century. On the one hand, there were those who disparaged "area studies," claiming that all the focus on language and culture by area study centers was passé, and could easily be replaced by a one-size-fits-all global studies curriculum that could function largely out of the power language of English. At the same time, the cross-disciplinary constituency of area study centers anticipated in many ways the growing commitment to interdisciplinarity or transdisciplinarity in American higher education. Caught between these quite different negating and affirming agendas, international study at ASU in the last quarter of the twentieth century benefited, quite unintentionally, from the hire of a surprisingly large number of Russian and East European specialists in a variety of disciplines ranging from economics, political science, history, religious studies, and musicology to language and literature. These disciplines in their hiring were responding no doubt to the popularity of Soviet studies at a time of dramatic geo-political transformation that included the fall of the Berlin Wall in 1989 and the collapse of the former Soviet Union in 1991. The story of Russian and East European studies

---

New York: The Armenian Center, Columbia University, 1986.
2. The Melikian Center title began to be used from December 2006 when Emma and Gregory Melikian first transferred funds into the Melikian family endowment at the ASU Foundation. The formal signing of the agreement and opening dinner reception followed in February 2007.

at Arizona State University is the account of how these relatively new faculty members began to act in concert to build a national program that could capture the imagination not just of national grant program officers, but of community leaders such as Emma and Gregory Melikian.

The building process involved three critical commitments that came to distinguish Eurasian and East European study at ASU. The first of these, chronologically, was the commitment to international educational partnerships and academic exchange. This was inspired in the first instance by a contribution from an anonymous Tempe donor (later determined to be the father of Economics Department Professor Marvin Jackson) to launch an academic exchange with the University of SS. Kiril and Metodij (UKIM) in Skopje, Macedonia. The donation in 1973 was tied to the City of Tempe's adoption of Skopje as a sister city—the first American adopted sister city to be located in a Communist country—what was then Yugoslavia.[3] In 1983, when ASU College of Liberal Arts and Sciences Dean Samuel Kirkpatrick authorized funding for the Russian and East European Studies Consortium (REESC), part of that funding was to provide annual support for a UKIM exchangee at ASU. When ASU President Lattie Coor in 1998 traveled to Macedonia to mark the 25th anniversary of the ASU-UKIM exchange in the newly independent Republic of Macedonia (subsequently North Macedonia), he met with more than one-hundred Macedonian UKIM colleagues who had benefitted from the exchange. At a public reception hosted by U.S. Ambassador to Macedonia Christopher Hill, Coor heralded the importance of such exchanges for international understanding and for international security. Inter-university partnerships would become a hallmark of the Melikian Center, growing to more than ten affiliations with Eurasian and East European institutions—welcoming international colleagues, opening study abroad opportunities for ASU students, and creating research pathways for ASU faculty members.[4]

---

3. The ASU-UKIM exchange was initially launched under the direction of an ASU sociologist, Scott McNall, who left ASU later to become provost and interim president of California State University at Chico. When McNall left ASU in 1975, *ad hoc* annual arrangements were made for placement of an annual UKIM exchangee with the help of ASU Professor Peter Horwath.
4. ASU REESC international partners included, in the first instance, those institutions cooperating on major U.S. State Department and USAID projects for curricular reform and international development—University of SS. Kiril and Metodij (Skopje, Macedonia), Lomonosov State University (Moscow, Russia), Yerevan State University (Armenia), University of Prishtina (Kosovo), University of Sarajevo (Bosnia & Herzegovina), and Il'ia State University (Georgia). In addition, ASU's Critical Languages Institute drew faculty

A second focal point for ASU Eurasian and East European area faculty naturally became that of building the infrastructure for regional studies within the university. This would ultimately involve development and recruitment of faculty affiliates, but the initial focus became that of the ASU University Libraries. As early as 1977, ASU faculty members who worked with Russian sources met with ASU Director of Libraries Donald Koepp (later the librarian of Princeton University) to secure regular Russian publications for ASU Libraries. One of the outcomes of those meetings was the launch of a regular "blanket order" for receipt of current Russian publications from the Soviet Union, first organized through Four Continents Book Corporation in New York City. That was followed by a faculty-managed sponsorship of six journals formerly published at Pittsburgh University under the editorship of the entrepreneurial Charles Schlacks, Jr. (*Canadian-American Slavic Studies; Russian History; Soviet Studies; Southeastern Europe; East-Central Europe,* and *Byzantine Studies*).[5] The journals and their editor moved to ASU in 1977. By 1980, ASU Libraries routinely received at no cost on exchange more serial publications from East European and Soviet institutions than any other university in the American southwest.[6]

The third and by far the most important set of initiatives launched by ASU faculty in East European and Eurasian studies were the measures undertaken to benefit ASU students. Starting in 1983, the Russian and East European Studies Consortium introduced a certificate program geared to honor students who, alongside their degree in a major field, could receive

---

from and placed its students in the following partner institutions: University of Tirana (Albania), Adam Mickiewicz University (Poznan, Poland), Kazan State University (Russia), and Tashkent State Pedagogical University (Uzbekistan), among others.

5. The journals' publication was overseen by a four-member ASU Russian and East European Publication (REEP) board consisting of Professor Frederick Giffin (History), Josef Brada (Economics), Lee Croft (Department of Languages and Literatures), and Stephen Batalden, chair (History). When the Schlacks journals moved to ASU from the University of Pittsburgh, they had been chronically late in meeting publication deadlines. Although the journals were brought up-to-date during their brief stay at ASU, ASU sponsorship of the Schlacks journals was terminated in the 1980s following administrative charges brought against the editor. Charles Schlacks died in 2022, but several of the Schlacks journals continue to be published under new editorship at Brill publishing house headquartered in Leiden, The Netherlands.

6. The ASU Library hired its first Slavic-area librarian in 1978 as a "Slavic Exchange Librarian," a post first held by Sandra Batalden. Following discontinuation of the exchange of journals, the position became that of a Slavic acquisitions librarian. Others holding that position have included Molly Molloy (later a Slavic librarian at Stanford University), Michael Markiw, and Alexandra Humphries, the current holder of the position.

a transcripted "Certificate in Russian and East European Studies." It was at the time of its origins the most rigorous program of its kind in international studies at ASU, requiring a minimum of three years' study of an East European or Eurasian language, plus an additional thirty semester credit hours of interdisciplinary coursework.

In the summer of 1991, with a grant from the American Council of Learned Societies, the Consortium began to offer intensive instruction in two less-commonly taught languages of the region, Serbo-Croatian (Bosnian/Croatian/Serbian[BCS]) and Macedonian. Throughout the 1990s, the number of languages and the number of students (both ASU and non-ASU) enrolled in the program grew significantly. In 1992, the summer program assumed the name it holds today, the ASU Critical Languages Institute (CLI). The commitment to the CLI, while it stemmed from a broad interest in empowering students, was very much tied to the end of the Cold War and the collapse of the Soviet Union. There had always been the canard that drew would-be spies into Russian language study—namely, "you need to know Russian to know the enemy." Such Cold War jingoism, needlessly derogatory, was plainly counter-productive by the 1990s, when needed expertise on the post-Soviet world required graduates with proficiency not just in Russian, but also in other official languages of the region, such as Ukrainian, Armenian, Macedonian, Tatar, Albanian, and Uzbek. Moreover, there were special advantages to be had for ASU students if they undertook non-Russian language training. New government support for study abroad alongside the traditional Fulbright Program—notably, the Boren National Security Education Program (NSEP) that began in 1991 as a Congressional post-Cold War peace dividend extracted out of the Defense Department budget—offered competitive advantages to both undergraduate and graduate students who demonstrated promise in prior study of a non-Russian Eurasian or East European language. At ASU, except for the CLI, Russian remained until 2000 the only Slavic language taught in the regular ASU academic-year curriculum. The CLI, by offering a program of expanded summer training in non-Russian languages of Eurasia and Eastern Europe, helped to generate an unusually large number of national Boren and Fulbright fellows (more than 150 such awards granted to CLI graduates since 1991).

Today, owing to expanded external grant support, generous scholarship assistance, a remarkable succession of CLI directors, a distinguished faculty of summer language instructors, and a dedicated support staff, the ASU Critical Languages Institute is now one of the nation's premier summer language institutes for less commonly taught languages of Eastern Europe and Eurasia. In 2023, the CLI offered intensive beginning and advanced summer language training in more than a dozen languages, ranging alphabetically from Albanian and Armenian to Tatar and Uzbek. Over the course of its 33-year history, the Critical Languages Institute has benefited from the leadership of seven directors[7] and more than two-dozen world-class native-speaker language instructors, among them some of the most distinguished language pedagogues of the region.[8] In recognition of its academic contribution to the university and its portfolio of annual external grants and contracts, the Russian and East European Studies Consortium was accorded center status in 2003 ("Russian and East European Studies Center") within the ASU College of Liberal Arts and Sciences (CLAS), ultimately assuming its university name as The Melikian Center in December

7. The founding director of the ASU Critical Languages Institute was ASU Russian Language and Literature Professor Lee B. Croft, who wrote the initial grant proposals and helped secure the CLI student tuition waiver as an ASU institutional match to external grant funding provided by the American Council of Learned Societies (ACLS) and the Social Sciences Research Council (SSRC). That original ACLS and SSRC external grant support has now been superseded by direct funding from the U.S. Department of State's Title VIII program. Professor Croft served as CLI director until 1997 when, at his request and with the agreement of the then chair of the ASU Department of Languages and Literatures David Foster, the CLI was moved directly under the Russian and East European Studies Consortium whose director, Stephen Batalden, also assumed the directorship of the CLI (1997-2002). From 2002, the CLI benefited from the hire of full-time directors, including distinguished linguists Danko Sipka (2002-2005), Ariana Stern-Gottschalk (2006-2009), and Kathleen Evans-Romaine (2009-2017). Most recently, the CLI has continued to grow under the direction of two talented anthropologists, Irina Levin (2018-2022) and Jamie Edmonds (2023 -). Excellent support personnel—starting with Patricia Nay, and continuing with Carol Withers, Susan Edgington, David Brokaw, Philip Carrano, and Marina Akins—were critical in managing the growth of the CLI over its first twenty-five years.
8. Several CLI instructors have published their own authoritative language textbooks. A few have served as CLI faculty members for more than twenty years. Illustrative of the dedication and academic standing of these CLI instructors is the case of Linda Meniku (ASU and University of Tirana), a veteran of more than 25 CLI summer institutes who has not only single-handedly generated more Fulbright and Boren/NSEP fellows for advanced study in Albania and Kosovo than any other Albanian program in the United States, but has also written the definitive modern Albanian texts and accompanying workbooks (*Discovering Albanian* and *Colloquial Albanian,* University of Wisconsin Press, 2011, 2012). Although there has been some natural turnover within the CLI instructional corps, among the longest serving distinguished colleagues who have built the CLI language programs in their respective native languages are Gohar Harutyunyan (Yerevan State University, Armenian), Agnieszka Mielczarek (Adam Mickiewicz University, Polish), and Saodat Adilova (Tashkent State Pedagogical University, Uzbek).

2006. Within CLAS, the Melikian Center director continues to report to the dean of Social Sciences.[9]

Emma Melikian's contact with Russian, Eurasian, and East European studies at ASU dates from the early 1990s. Her eldest son James had been an ASU history baccalaureate major and a student of Russian, taking area-related coursework in Russian and East European Studies. But Emma's first direct contact with the ASU Russian and East European Studies faculty dated from the 1990s when ASU colleagues participated in the annual Thank You America Festival of Nations. There followed occasions with visiting delegations from Eurasia when Emma would join ASU faculty members, invariably assisting when Russian translation was needed. That all changed when, in 2001, the Russian and East European Studies Consortium's director Stephen Batalden and faculty affiliate Victor Agadjanian met at the San Carlos Hotel with the Melikians to discuss the prospect of adding Eastern Armenian to the languages taught in the Critical Languages Institute. There followed an ASU proposal prepared by Consortium Director Batalden to Emma and Gregory Melikian in the fall of 2000 seeking Melikian financial support ($30,000) for a three-year pilot effort to integrate Armenian into the CLI.

When no word was forthcoming from the Melikians about the proposal, Batalden asked Agadjanian, an ASU sociologist at the time, if he might inquire when he next saw the Melikians at the Armenian Cultural Center about their interest in the proposal. Emma recalls Professor Agadjanian coming up to her to inquire about the matter, and her surprise when he mentioned a proposal she had never seen. Having hand-delivered the proposal to Gregory Melikian at the San Carlos Hotel, the ASU colleagues had assumed that the proposal, addressed to both Emma and Gregory, would reach both parties. What followed was instructive about the management of philanthropy within the Melikian family. Within a week of the Agadjanian query at the Armenian Cultural Center, Batalden received word from Emma that the Melikians were indeed ready to support the Armenian program in the ASU Critical Languages Institute. The problem had not been

---

9. The continuity and strength in the office of the Melikian Center director has been particularly notable, including three distinguished interim directors (Kathleen Evans-Romaine, Mark von Hagen, and Craig Calhoun). The current director Keith Brown (2017 -), who has authored the Center's first successful USDE Title VI National Resource Center grant, assumed his position following the one-year interim appointment of the late Mark von Hagen.

a lack of Gregory Melikian's support for the effort—he may well have welcomed the proposal, which nevertheless sat on his desk at the San Carlos Hotel. The issue instead was that on matters of such cultural investment Emma was the one who typically exercised leadership.

There followed a formal announcement of the first Melikian Fund at the ASU Foundation, and a luncheon in February 2001 honoring Emma and Gregory Melikian at the ASU University Club—a luncheon hosted by then ASU President Lattie Coor. Following the search for an instructor in Eastern Armenian, the first intensive summer course in Eastern Armenian commenced in the 2001 Critical Languages Institute with twelve students. An instructor had been recruited from Yerevan State University—an Armenian language philologist Arousiak Gevorkian who had published her own elementary Armenian textbook.

It is a credit to the CLI and to Emma that the Armenian program managed to withstand its first two difficult years. As fate would have it, the initial Armenian instructor failed to generate student interest. And, as if that were not problem enough, she was initially accompanied into the classroom by her husband who proceeded to laugh at the awkward pronunciation of beginning students, most of whom were of non-Armenian parentage—an embarrassment for all concerned. Batalden, who was CLI director at the time, was mortified, and feared that nothing would come of the effort to launch Armenian in the CLI. Emma, who had encouraged her own sons to join the Armenian course in the CLI, was remarkably patient, only expressing her utter dismay when the couple, after having been relieved of instructional responsibilities at the CLI, violated the terms of their visas, remaining in the United States (in Los Angeles) where they became *de facto* undocumented aliens—the only such instance of visa abuse in the thirty-three-year history of the ASU Critical Languages Institute.

Remarkably, by 2003, the Armenian program not only was able to be resuscitated, but in the process the ASU relationship with Yerevan State University broadened into a major inter-university partnership. In the fall of 2002, during his visit to Yerevan State University, Batalden conducted first-person interviews with candidates for the Armenian instructional position in the CLI. Out of those interviews, two talented Armenian philologists from the YSU Faculty of Philology, both of whom were teachers of English, not Armenian, emerged to guide the future success of Armenian in the CLI for more than a generation. The first of those, Siranush

Khandanyan, began instruction in Armenian in the summer 2003 CLI. She would soon be followed by her YSU colleague Gohar Harutyunyan. The two split the teaching responsibilities, with a second-year program beginning already in 2004. Among the successful graduates of this expanded Armenian program in the CLI were five students—none of Armenian parentage—who would later receive national Boren scholarships for study abroad in Armenia.[10] In effect, Emma's patience in building the Armenian program in the ASU Critical Languages Institute had been and continues to be rewarded. Khandanyan and Harutyunyan not only put the Armenian program on a solid footing, but while doing so they were enlisted by Emma into co-curricular engagements within the wider Armenian community of greater Phoenix.

The fall 2002 travel of Batalden to Armenia was not only for the purpose of interviewing potential CLI instructors. It also was a site visit to ready ASU's application for State Department (DoS) funding for a curricular reform project linking ASU with Yerevan State University. The $250,000 project, funded by the DoS Bureau of Educational and Cultural Affairs, was for the development of a new public administration program at YSU modeled after a comparable graduate Master of Public Administration program at the ASU School of Public Affairs. Public administration in the former Soviet Union had traditionally been viewed as an extension of administrative law, often at the expense of politicizing the discipline. This first direct ASU-YSU partnership project, in seeking to institute a new MPA program at Yerevan State University, sought to liberate public administration from administrative law by refashioning the program as a social science discipline with practical career training objectives. As in subsequent curricular partnership projects conducted by the ASU Melikian Center with many Eurasian and East European universities, the project methodology entailed extended semester-in-residence visits of carefully selected YSU faculty members who attended regular ASU graduate seminars and prepared syllabi for new coursework to be launched at YSU.

---

10. Among the earliest in this cohort was ASU undergraduate history major, Erin Hutchinson, who followed her Boren Award with a Fulbright fellowship to Moldova, a graduate fellowship to Harvard University where she completed her Ph.D. in Eurasian history, and an appointment in the University of Colorado History Department where she is currently an assistant professor of Russian and Eurasian history. Emma takes great interest in following the careers of such CLI students, particularly in the case of those studying Russian, Armenian, and Farsi—the languages Emma herself commands.

The public administration project at YSU succeeded even beyond expectations, and it continues twenty years later to be a model for curricular reform in the post-Soviet world. Much of the success of these programs in Armenia rests on the leadership of key project partners at Yerevan State University—notably, Dr. Alexander Markarov who for more than a generation has headed the YSU International Office in the university's rectorate. But another significant reason for the success of such projects has been the intangible contributions—the human dimension—of international scholarly exchange. At that level, Emma Ordjanian Melikian was a special gift to the project, as she would be in all comparable efforts. The Melikian home became a welcoming site for visiting scholars. When the project's YSU director (Markarov) visited ASU, accompanied by YSU Rector (University President) Radik Martirosyan, Emma hosted a dinner in the rector's honor, the first of four such current and former YSU university rectors hosted in the Melikian home. At the close of each semester when successive cohorts of visiting YSU scholars presented their draft syllabi at an ASU event, Emma was in the front row, masking her pride in their achievements as she asked her own pointed questions of the visitors.

For Emma Ordjanian Melikian, although she may not have expressed it, there was the dawning awareness that she was, in fact, a shareholder in an expanded program of international educational exchange and partnership that linked her love of America and American institutions with a desire to contribute to the advancement of the lands and people she had left behind. What had begun as a modest financial effort to introduce Eastern Armenian into the Critical Languages Institute had mushroomed into a grant-funded international program empowering students and faculty both at ASU and at Yerevan State University in Armenia. Inspired by the initial pilot Melikian Fund at ASU for Armenian, the national Social Science Research Council began to provide annual funding for Armenian in the CLI in 2003. In effect, the ASU partnership with YSU and the CLI's Armenian instruction, although separately funded, had begun to build upon each other, and upon the foundation laid by Melikian support.

It was in such a context that the ASU Center Director Batalden in 2005 first broached with his Social Sciences Dean, Alan Artibise, the idea of naming the ASU Russian, Eurasian, and East European Studies Center for the Melikian family. Naming rights at Arizona State University involve provision of much larger endowment support, but Artibise took the matter under consideration. Among the hurdles that needed to be surmounted was an internal review within the ASU Foundation to determine whether there were other units of the university that might take priority in any such larger appeal to the Melikians.

These issues came to a head in the summer of 2006 when Batalden and Artibise joined in a contentious meeting at the ASU Foundation with other key foundation administrators. At the meeting there was mention of Melikian family support for the public television station KAET-TV at ASU, for the ASU School of Music, and for the School of Public Affairs in downtown Phoenix— one foundation executive noting the proximity of the School of Public Affairs to the Melikians' San Carlos Hotel. Dean Artibise, clearly exasperated by the di-

Dean Alan Artibise

rection of the discussion, turned to the group in his characteristically direct, straightforward manner, saying as best as can be recalled:

> Ok, which one of you volunteers to go to Emma and tell her that she should be less interested in the training of students taking place in the Critical Languages Institute, or that she should be less interested in the study of Russia, Armenia, or Persia? I don't see any volunteers, because none of you know the family. Unless I hear otherwise, Steve and I will be glad to approach Gregory and Emma Melikian about this naming opportunity on behalf of the Russian and East European Studies Center.

That said, the meeting closed shortly thereafter, and Alan Artibise instructed Batalden to prepare some initial wording for an appeal to the Melikians. In private conversations, Gregory and Emma had seemed genuinely pleased that there was interest in honoring them in this way, but of course they were wanting to know how they could make that happen.

Later that same fall of 2006, Dean Artibise and Center Director Batalden met with the Melikians at their home, bringing a proposal from the

ASU Foundation for the endowment of what was to be named "The Melikian Center for Russian, Eurasian, & East European Studies," or more simply, The Melikian Center. While the Melikians were given time to consider the matter, the response from Gregory and Emma was almost immediate and positive, including their pledge of an initial endowment of $1 million dollars, and assistance to the Melikian Center in raising a second million—a figure that has now been exceeded. Emma recalls how there was little discussion over the matter. It was something they both wanted to do, and the recent sale of their home and adjoining property on Arcadia Drive had yielded liquid assets more than sufficient to meet such a commitment. Although the signatures of Emma and Gregory Melikian were not affixed to the ASU Foundation agreement until February 2007, when a dinner was held in their honor, the first installment toward the endowment of The Melikian Center was received by the ASU Foundation in December 2006. Thus, the Melikian Center naming can be considered to have been confirmed either in December 2006 or February 2007. What had begun as a modest effort to introduce Eastern Armenian into the ASU Critical Languages Institute had become six years later an endowed Melikian Center in the ASU College of Liberal Arts and Sciences. In recognition of this contribution to Arizona State University, Gregory and Emma Melikian were honored in 2010 as "Philanthropists of the Year" at the annual ASU Founders' Day Award Ceremony.

Photo of Emma and Gregory Melikian on the occasion of their receipt of the "Philanthropists of the Year" Award at the 2010 ASU Founders' Day Ceremony. Photo courtesy of ASU Alumni Association.

In the months and years that followed the founding of The Melikian Center there were at least three distinct ways in which Emma continued to drive the Center's agenda—as an outreach advocate expanding the footprint of the Center; as a champion, more specifically, of the Critical Languages Institute; and finally, as a global ambassador leveraging her own and Gregory Melikian's donor status on behalf of the Center's partnerships with overseas institutions.

As outreach advocate, Emma consistently sought to expand the audience for Center programming, seeking, for example, greater Center and CLI engagement with high school students. The hire of the Center's first outreach coordinator, Andrew Gunn, in 2015 was in part owing to the concerns of Emma for greater outreach to high school students who were gradually beginning to enroll in the CLI summer language offerings. Andrew Gunn would launch the Melikian Center's first successful Russian StarTalk grant, a program funded by the National Security Agency for K-12 summer language training in select languages (Arabic, Chinese, Persian, and Russian).[11]

The most obvious direct impact of Emma's outreach effort was her role in helping to create in 2013 the Melikian Center Advisory Board, a national board comprised of civic leaders, including some of ASU's own graduates in the field of Russian, Eurasian, and East European studies. More than half of the two dozen founding members of the Board have been friends or family of Emma and Gregory Melikian. Among the founding family members, for example, were Emma's son Robert Melikian, a practicing lawyer and historic site preservation-

Mary Karapetian Alvord

ist, and her niece Mary Alvord. Alvord, distinguished recipient of the 2020 Presidential Citation from the American Psychological Association, was the founder of Alvord, Baker and Associates, LLC, a group psychotherapy practice in Maryland. Advisory Board members, in addition to making an an-

---

11. On the StarTalk program at NSA, see their website, https://www.startalk.info/ (last accessed 2/19/2024).

nual contribution to the Melikian Center, have participated in overseas Melikian Center projects, have attended Center events on campus, have joined Center search committees, and have evaluated scholarship applications for the Critical Languages Institute.

The first president of the Advisory Board was Judge Charles G. Case, II, who alongside his duties in the U.S. Bankruptcy Court for the District of Arizona, had served on USAID judicial training projects in southeastern Europe. Among the distinguished successors to the Board presidency was Emma's own daughter, Ramona Melikian, a former Council on Foreign Relations officer and a professional consultant and corporate counselor specializing in the field of organizational psychology. Emma no doubt took pride in the important work of her daughter on behalf of the Melikian Center alongside her earlier work with the Thank You America Foundation. As appreciative as she was of the support of her own family and friends, Emma invariably mobilized this support from behind the scenes, deflecting attention from herself by praising the work of others for whom she set high standards. In such a manner the Melikian Center has benefited from the contributions of its Advisory Board members, and most especially from the strength and engagement of the Board's able leadership.[12]

Charles G. (Chuck) Case, II

Emma's role in the Center has also been focused on the Critical Languages Institute, whose teachers and students she champions. As one who speaks

Ramona Melikian

12. National Advisory Board members who have served on specific grant-funded overseas Center projects include Shahin Berisha, Ronald Birks, Philip Carrano, Charles Case, II, Lee Croft, Marcie Hutchinson, David Jankofsky, Ilene Lashinsky, David Merkel (current chair), the late J. Peter Morrow, and the late Walter Winius, Jr.

three of the languages taught in the Institute—Russian, Farsi, and Armenian—Emma has brought a level of linguistic expertise that is unique to the Center. Her bond with CLI instructors owes not just to her language skills, but also to her gracious welcome to these international scholars, especially to the women faculty members who comprise more than 75 percent of the instructional power of the Institute. As recently as the summer of 2023, Emma continued to host annual luncheons for members of the CLI faculty, many of whom she has come to know as friends over a period of ten or more summers. Similarly, Emma has been drawn to CLI students, some of whom have benefited from scholarships funded from the Melikian endowment, and several of whom correspond with Emma following their experiences overseas. Until recently, Emma has attended all the annual graduation ceremonies for the CLI, where students routinely ask to be photographed with her.

While such linkages with CLI faculty and students quite obviously are mutually reinforcing, Emma's behind-the-scenes role in assuring the continuity and authority of the CLI has been less well understood. As noted above, in 1997, with the support of the chair of the ASU Department of Languages and Literatures (David Foster), the Critical Languages Institute formally moved its operations out of DLL and into the Russian and East European Studies Consortium at the time when DLL Professor Lee Croft stepped down from the CLI directorship. Much of the work of grant writing, student recruitment, and registration for the CLI had already moved to Russian and East European Studies by that time, but the importance of the change was that course prefixes (such as RUS 100 or BCS 101) would for the first time be shared by a unit (Russian and East European Studies) that was outside DLL and outside of the Humanities Division of the College of Liberal Arts and Sciences (there are three divisions within CLAS, each with its own dean—Humanities, Social Sciences, and Natural Sciences). For historical reasons, most area-study centers, such as The Melikian Center, have always been located within the Social Sciences, rather than the Humanities, division.

In the years since 1997 when the transfer of the CLI became formalized, there have occasionally been what might best be called "turf conflicts." Even though the DLL and its successor School of International Letters and Cultures (SILC) were not equipped to handle the administrative detail entailed in annual CLI grant writing, overseas contract negotiation, student recruitment, and registration, DLL and SILC administrators have occasionally looked with envy at CLI grants and enrollment, and have questioned whether "their" prefixes ought to be able to be used for Melikian Center CLI language courses in a college other than that of the Humanities. At some point in this ongoing discussion, the SILC director, with support from his Humanities dean, secured College-level authority to require Melikian Center annual payment to SILC for summer revenue (funds distributed each year by ASU Summer Sessions to units of the university offering summer courses). This was annual summer revenue that, SILC argued, was being "lost" to the Melikian Center by virtue of the CLI's appropriation of "their" language course prefixes and course listings. The resulting annual burden upon the Melikian Center became part of doing business in the College, even though the grant-funded CLI courses provided tuition waivers for CLI students, such that no comparable ASU Summer Sessions revenue was being paid to the Melikian Center to offset the SILC surcharge.

The subject of this annual multi-thousand-dollar surcharge levied upon the Melikian Center by SILC (a surcharge by one ASU unit levied against another ASU unit) and the "turf conflict" that this represented became major subjects of consideration at the annual meeting in 2011, a meeting the Melikian Center staff hosted for Melikian family each December for a program review. Emma Melikian was rightly concerned to learn about these "turf conflicts," making it clear to all attending that something needed to be done to assure the integrity and authority of the Critical Languages Institute and its place in the Melikian Center. Present at the meeting was the ASU Social Sciences Dean Linda Lederman, whose collegial support for the Melikian Center was doubly reinforced by a personal friendship she had developed with Emma Melikian.

Adding to Emma's concern at the meeting was the discovery that the original agreement signed by Gregory and Emma Melikian with the ASU Foundation in February 2007 made no explicit reference to the Critical Languages Institute. The Melikian endowment agreement established only The Melikian Center, leaving understood, but unwritten, the status of the Critical Languages Institute as an integral part of Melikian Center operations. Emma's concern, forcefully presented, was that absent any explicit reference to the Critical Languages Institute as a unit of the Melikian Center, the decision of 1997 to move the CLI under Russian and East European Studies could conceivably be reversed by some willful future ASU administrator.

Linda Lederman understood and sympathized with Emma's clearly articulated concern. To address the situation, Dean Lederman offered to approach the ASU Foundation with the goal of inserting language into the Melikian agreement clarifying that the Melikian Endowment explicitly supports the ASU Critical Languages Institute which is and will continue to be an integral part of the Melikian Center. Although ASU Foundation agreements with donors are "never" to be changed, this language change, thanks to the persistence of Emma Melikian and the sup-

Dean Linda Lederman

port of Dean Lederman, was adopted by the ASU Foundation in a revised agreement signed by Emma and Gregory Melikian on January 6, 2012. Disappointingly, the multi-thousand-dollar surcharge levied annually by SILC upon the Melikian Center's Critical Languages Institute nevertheless remains in place. What the discussion over "turf conflict" revealed was how seriously Emma Ordjanian Melikian took her identification with and engagement in the Critical Languages Institute.

While Emma understood the limits of her ability to effect change in a large bureaucratic institution such as Arizona State University, she also knew how best to leverage Melikian endowments. This became important not just for the advancement of the Critical Languages Institute, but also for productive ties with regions of the world where her own family has had deep roots. Twenty years ago Emma was drawn to the Melikian Center as much for its partnership activity in Armenia with Yerevan State University as for the support of American students in the CLI. Those partnerships continued, and she has remained engaged, following each new partnership, whether it was with post-graduate fellows from Sarajevo coming to build a new master's degree in religious studies at the University of Sarajevo, young faculty from Kosovo coming to build new curriculum in accountancy at the University of Prishtina, or women colleagues from Armenia coming to launch a new Center for Gender and Leadership Studies at Yerevan State University.

What Emma Ordjanian Melikian had come to realize was that creative area-study university centers, such as the Melikian Center, could not only advance student understanding of critical languages and regions of the world—including in this case a region in which she had been born and raised—but could also engage in the kind of overseas international development that could be educationally and economically transformative.

Recognizing the power that comes with leveraging philanthropy for such transformative change in Eurasia, Emma Ordjanian Melikian has most recently developed a vision for one more legacy contribution as she enters her tenth decade. Borrowing on the work of Melikian Center faculty affiliate, Professor Visar Berisha, and his project in southeastern Europe, Emma has set her sights on replicating Berisha's entrepreneurship project for Armenia and potentially other parts of Eurasia. The Berisha project, "GIST Innovates the Balkans," is a State Department-funded project designed to train young entrepreneurs who are developing their own businesses in Serbia, Bosnia and Herzegovina, Kosovo, Albania, and North Macedonia, helping them to secure western capital, develop usable business skills, design workable business plans, and produce products in cutting-edge fields of science and technology. GIST is a broader State Department acronym used for projects that help develop "Global Innovation in Science and Technology."[13]

When Emma learned of the Berisha project, her immediate thought was that the project was one that could readily be replicated in other front-line post-Soviet economies, notably in the Republic of Armenia. Not only is such innovative entrepreneurship training in applied science and technology needed in such emerging economies, but her thought was that some of the would-be entrepreneurs might actually come out of another partnership that the Melikian Center currently supports with Yerevan State University—namely, a partnership in American Studies that has helped launch the YSU American Studies Center with its own degree program. What better way to memorialize the Ordjanian legacy and the remarkable entrepreneurship of her Russian-Persian-Armenian father Samson than to support young, uncorrupted entrepreneurs who are building a new world in post-Soviet Armenia. To that end, and with an eye toward enlisting wider family and friends in the effort, she is laying the groundwork for the

---

13. For a GIST program overview, see the website, https://wwtnetwork.org/activity/gist-innovates-balkans-2024 (last accessed 2/19/2024).

Ordjanian-Odjaghian-Melikian Fund at the Melikian Center—the OOM acronym conveniently yielding the Cyrillic sound *um* (the Russian root word for "mind" or "intellect").

For Emma Ordjanian Melikian this latest venture is part of what she means when she says, "I am a grateful Persian-Armenian immigrant in twenty-first century America, having lived in two centuries, within four [Russian, Persian, Armenian, and American] great cultures."

Afterword from Emma Ordjanian Melikian

I am overcome with deep gratitude to Steve Batalden for his time and countless travels to pen this book, and to his wife Sandy Batalden for her invaluable editing skills that have brought this project to life.

Words cannot adequately express my gratitude to my father, Samson Ordjanian, who selflessly supported our family from the tender age of twelve when he first traveled to Russia to earn a living, and to my mother, Maria Rustamian, who tirelessly nurtured and cared for our extended family in Russia and beyond.

To my dearly departed siblings I owe an immense debt of gratitude. My brother Nikit Ordjanian not only lovingly assumed the role of head of family after the untimely passing of our father but he also later began to document our family history. My dear sister Isabella became a second mother to me after the passing of our mother Maria. And brother Ashot, who died too young, gave me the love of music, for which I am forever grateful.

To my loving husband of 70 years, Gregory J. Melikian, who embarked on countless adventures with me and helped me truly savor life, I offer a heartfelt thank you.

Special recognition goes to my children: my son, James, who displayed an innate penchant for history from the very moment he entered this world; my son, Robert, a steadfast lawyer who has always been there for our family and for whom I express my deepest gratitude; my son, Richard, whose skilled hands can mend anything and who taught me the true meaning of quiet acts of charity; and a special word to my daughter, Ramona, who has been a source of joy and blessing every single day of her life. Thank you all.

To my amazing and steadfast daughters-in-law, Nevine and Ana, who have brought love and life to our family, and to my cherished grandchildren, Alexandra, Arra, and Isabella, who constantly make me burst with pride, I am eternally grateful for your presence in my life.

I would also like to extend my heartfelt thanks to my extended family and cousins around the globe, whose unwavering love and support continually uplift me, especially my nieces, Elsa, Mary, Anahid, and Armen who carry our family legacy with pride.

Gratitude is also owed to Father Zacharia Saribekyan and the St. Apkar Armenian Apostolic Church and Cultural Center of Arizona, along with our resilient community, for their indispensable contributions in constructing our cherished church, both in a physical and emotional sense.

Lastly, a profound thank you is extended to all those involved with the Thank You America Foundation of Arizona and The Melikian Center for Russian, Eurasian & East European Studies at Arizona State University.

May God shower you all with His blessings and take care of each and every one of you.

With all my love and deep appreciation,
Emma Ordjanian Melikian
Phoenix, AZ, USA April 2024
frompersiatoamerica.com

About the Author

Stephen K. Batalden is professor emeritus of history and founding director of the Melikian Center for Russian, Eurasian and East European Studies at Arizona State University. A specialist on Russian and East European religious and cultural history, his Cambridge University Press volume, *Russian Bible Wars: Modern Scriptural Translation and Cultural Authority*, received the 2014 Reginald Zelnik Award of the Association for Slavic, East European, and Eurasian Studies for outstanding contribution to modern Russian history.

Index

9 798385 129720